**"Produced by special arrangement with
Original Works Publishing."**
www.originalworksonline.com

Good Mourning, America
Third Printing, 2008
Fourth Printing, 2010
Printed in U.S.A.
ISBN 978-1-934962-11-4

Blinders
by Patrick Gabridge

3 Males, 1 Female, 4 Chorus Members

Synopsis: Scientists announce that they have found two people who are exactly alike. Not twins, but two identical human beings. Pulitzer Prize winning reporter, Karen Sayer can clearly see that the "duplicates," Chris and Alex, look absolutely nothing alike. No one else seems to notice, or care, and the media unleashes a feeding frenzy over the new scientific discovery. With modern science and the media behind them Chris and Alex are catapulted to instant celebrity. With the help of Karen's salesman fiancé Stack, the incredible identicals campaign for the Presidency under the slogan "Two Heads Are Better Than One." Knowing she must do something to awaken the world, Karen is suddenly thrust to the forefront of an assassination attempt. Will she have the courage to follow through? Will she succeed before it's too late? Only the outrageous conclusion holds the answers.

Junk Bonds
by Lucy Wang

5 Males, 1 Female

Synopsis: In a fast-paced game of liar's poker a young Asian American woman fights her way into the clubby, high rolling world of Wall Street. Immense wealth, glamorous careers and intoxicating power are at stake in pursuit of a fat slice of
American pie.

GOOD MOURNING, AMERICA

**A Play By
Lucy Wang**

PLAYERS

Minimum Cast = 8
With Actors Playing Multiple Roles

KATIE
FLIGHT ATTENDANT
DANA
ALEX
SUSAN
MOURNERS
PATIENTS
GEORGE "DUBYA" BUSH - voiceover
PROFESSOR PHILIP MADDEN
MARK
ROY (female who changed her name from Helen, not a transvestite/
transsexual)
ASPCA REP
TORI
CHRIS
OKLAHOMA BOMBING SURVIVOR (female)
FIREMAN'S PREGNANT WIDOW
21 YEAR OLD
ASIAN AMERICAN
POLICE OFFICER
HERVÉ - French, "H" is silent
VENDORS
HENRY as ANNA
DOCTORS
JOY
KATIE'S MOM (BARBARA)
MARY
THERON
YOUNG SOLDIER

/ denotes overlapping dialogue

ONE DOUBLING PROPOSAL

ALEX
KATIE
DANA

- GEORGE "DUBYA" BUSH/PROFESSOR MADDEN/POLICE OFFICER/HERVÉ
- SUSAN/VENDOR/MOURNER/FIREMAN'S PREGNANT WIDOW/PATIENT/ROY
- CHRIS/YOUNG SOLDIER/MOURNER/VENDOR/ASPCA REP/PATIENT/HENRY AS ANNA
- TORI/ OKLAHOMA BOMBING SURVIVOR/KATIE'S MOM/ MARY/PATIENT/JOY
- FLIGHT ATTENDANT/ASIAN AMERICAN/THERON/ DOCTOR/MARK/21 YEAR OLD

ACKNOWLEDGEMENTS

I would like to thank the following people for helping make GOOD MOURNING, AMERICA possible.

Eric Bogosian for urging me to transform my pain, losses and true stories into this play.

The Atlantic Center of the Arts for allowing us to form Bogo Rep and, thus, for being one of the best artistic residencies ever.

The illustrious members of Bogo Rep for taking the journey: Beau Allulli, Rob Anderson, Gideon Banner, Nikole Beckwith, Elliotte Crowell, Jennifer Gibbs, Josh Lefkowitz, Greg McCain, and Sarah Utterback.

Rob Urbinati and Jeff Rosenstock for being the first to present a staged reading of GOOD MOURNING, AMERICA before live New York audiences.

To the victims and survivors of 9/11 for sharing their heartaches and truths.

Finally, this play is for Tom Halpern whose love and luminosity open new worlds, and help me glow in the dark.

Good Mourning, America

ACT ONE

THE CALL TO CONSCIOUSNESS

SCENE 1

SETTING: Los Angeles International Airport, AKA LAX.
AT RISE: KATIE arrives at the gate with her carry-on and laptop.
She hands her ticket to the FLIGHT ATTENDANT.

KATIE: Hi, my name is Katie Fields.

FLIGHT ATTENDANT: Welcome!

KATIE: *(Directly to AUDIENCE.)* The journey we're about to take really happened. To me. True stories. Sure, identities have been doctored and compressed to protect the beautiful and the damned. Dramatic license issued, suspended, renewed, revoked. Civil and uncivil liberties taken, stolen, ravaged.   But no way could I ever have imagined this all on my own.   Never in a million years. And yet, it really happened. To me.

FLIGHT ATTENDANT: Good afternoon, ladies and gentlemen, this is your final boarding call for American Airlines Flight Number 212, with nonstop service from Los Angeles to New York. Please have your boarding passes out.

KATIE: *(Directly to AUDIENCE.)* Ready for take-off? Seat upright, baggage stowed safely beneath the person in front of you? Brace yourself, truth has a tendency to shift unexpectedly during flight.

KATIE hands FLIGHT ATTENDANT her boarding pass and boards the plane.

SCENE 2

SETTING: New York, September 10, 2001, evening, ALEX and DANA's penthouse apartment. Tribeca.
AT RISE: ALEX watches TV with a TiVo remote while DANA, nervous, tidies up.

ALEX: I wish you'd stop fussing.   The place sparkles.

DANA: I hope when Katie arrives, you'll turn off the TV.

ALEX: Why can't I watch TV?   What if I turn down the volume real low?

DANA: Can't we show a little class?   Just for tonight. One night.

ALEX: I thought Katie was your friend.

DANA: The best. We used to be best friends.

ALEX: Don't friends let friends watch TV?

DANA: At least turn the channel to PBS.   Alex, please, I want us to make a good impression.   Katie's so smart, so intellectual, I can't have her thinking we're blobs, couch potatoes.

ALEX: Katie's from L.A. Everyone in L.A. watches TV.

DANA: Please, Alex. For me?

ALEX: People who say they only watch PBS are full of shit. Liars.

Alex turns the channel to PBS.

ALEX: But I'll do it for you.

DANA: Just think how awesome it would be if Katie ends up winning a Pulitzer for a novel she wrote in our penthouse.

ALEX: That would be very cool.

DANA: Who knows?   Maybe she'd even thank us in her acknowledgements. "To Dana and Alex, who made it all possible."

ALEX: I always wanted to be famous, or know someone famous.

DANA: Please help me make Katie feel at home. Welcome.

ALEX: Don't worry.   I can't help noticing you grow more beautiful each passing day.

DANA: Alex.

ALEX: It's true.

DANA: You're right, watch whatever you want, true friends accept you for who you are. It's what's inside that counts.

Doorbell RINGS.

DANA: Sweetheart, will you get the door so I can check my face one more time? Pretty please.

ALEX: Of course.

ALEX starts for the door, but a sudden attack of sharp back pain stops him cold in his tracks.

ALEX: OUCH! Jesus H. Christ –

DANA: Your back?

ALEX: What else? Sorry. It comes and goes as it damn well pleases.

DANA: Oh, Alex, isn't there something more you can do? Take?

ALEX: Help me back to the couch? The good news, you look fantastic.

Doorbell RINGS.

DANA: Coming. *(To ALEX.)* You rest.

ALEX: I'm going nowhere.

DANA opens the front door.

DANA: Katie.

KATIE: Dana.

KATIE and DANA hug.

DANA: I can't believe you're really here.

KATIE: I know. Thanks for inviting me.

DANA: How was your flight?

KATIE: A little turbulent, but luckily, I got here in one piece. I probably have airplane hair.

DANA: You look great.

KATIE: So do you.

DANA: You look the same as you did senior year.

KATIE: God, I hope not, but I appreciate the sentiment.

DANA: I have your senior photo framed in the office.

KATIE: No way.

DANA: Way. I'll show you.

KATIE: How embarrassing. Dana. Why would you do that to me?

DANA: I've always loved that photograph.

ALEX: Hi. I'm Alex, Dana's husband.

DANA: Oh dear. Please forgive my manners.

KATIE: Nice to finally meet you.

ALEX: Likewise. I've heard so much about you. Is it all true? It's not all true, is it Katie?

KATIE: Why not? Works for Gore Vidal.

ALEX: No one could be that good. Could they?

DANA: If anyone can, Katie can. Back in high school, Katie was voted most likely to survive pestilence and famine.

KATIE: You remember that crap?

DANA: How could I forget?

ALEX: Well, I'll be. It is a pleasure and an honor.

LOUD THREATENING DOG BARKS.

KATIE: Oh my god, who or what is that?

DANA: Why, that's Gigi. We put her in our bedroom for now. Gigi loves to bounce all over newcomers.

KATIE: She doesn't sound quite as friendly as you described.

ALEX: Her bark is worse than her bite. Much worse.

DANA: Once she gets to know you, really know you –

ALEX: You'll be inseparable.

DANA: Want to meet her?

KATIE: Sure. Later.

ALEX: You must be thirsty. What can I get you? I'm afraid it has to be non-alcoholic.

DANA: Alex is in AA.

ALEX: Sorry to be such a drag.

KATIE: Ice tea, orange juice, whatever. All fine.

ALEX: Thanks. I'm on my merry way.

ALEX moves achingly. Lets out a few GROANS.

DANA: Oh sweetheart, I'll get the drinks. You sit and keep Katie company.

ALEX: Sorry, sweetheart.

KATIE: I can help.

ALEX: Please, you're our guest. You just arrived.

DANA: Alex suffers from chronic back pain. Tremendous back pain

KATIE: My back's started to hurt too. Occupational hazard for writers.

ALEX: I've been going to doctors three times a week for a year. Nothing.

KATIE: Yikes.

ALEX: Worse. I can't lift. I can barely move my right arm above my shoulder, or behind my back. I tire easily. There are days I can't even get up. I'm starting to lose faith in Western medicine.

KATIE: How awful. I'm sorry.

ALEX: My sponsor in A.A. is encouraging me to give acupuncture a try. But I don't know if I'm ready for needles.

KATIE: How are you going to get around in Italy?

ALEX: Italy's the most romantic place on earth. Capital R.

KATIE: Still, three weeks. Sure your back can handle that?

ALEX: A change of scenery can do wonders. But just to be safe, we're staying at luxury hotels just so we can avail ourselves of all the amenities.

KATIE: Of course.

ALEX: Plus I booked us on a bus tour. Found a bus with plush high back chairs. Cushiony. It's our <u>back</u> up plan.

KATIE: Clever.

ALEX: You have to be prepared.

DANA returns with some cold drinks.

DANA: Lemonade?

KATIE: Perfect.

ALEX: Thanks, sweetie. You're the best.

DANA: Alex and I want to thank you so much for house-sitting. We really appreciate you flying in all the way from Los Angeles.

KATIE: No sweat. What are friends for? Besides, how often does a struggling artist get offered the use of a two-story penthouse?

ALEX: A two-story penthouse with two terraces and two magnificent views.

KATIE: I feel like I won the lottery.

DANA: So you like?

KATIE: What's not to like?

DANA: So you think you can get a lot of writing done?

KATIE: I'll certainly try.

ALEX: What do you write? Tawdry romance novels?

KATIE: Hardly.

ALEX: No? Why not? They're my favorite.

DANA: Alex. Hacks write romance novels.

ALEX: They do? Sure fooled me. Then again, I've always been a sucker for a good romance. That's how Dana and I ended up together.

KATIE: Sounds sweet.

DANA: It was. Very.

ALEX: Whirlwind romance.

DANA: For the next three weeks, our home is your home. Invite as many or as few friends as you like. We trust you completely.

ALEX: Your husband Josh is welcome to visit too. We'd love to meet him. Some day.

KATIE: Thanks. I'm sure he'd love to come, but his job.

DANA: Manhattan is your oyster.

KATIE: I look forward to slurping away.

DANA: Lourdes normally comes in Tuesdays to clean. She'll do your laundry too, if you like.

KATIE: Wow, I'm impressed, I don't even have to clean up after myself. A sign you've really moved up in the world.

ALEX: Hey, from what Dana says, you deserve the best. She says you gave her sound financial advice.

DANA: How I miss those days.

KATIE: The market could have just as easily gone the other way.

DANA: But it didn't.

KATIE: If the market had turned the other way, who knows if I'd be sitting in your penthouse today.

ALEX: If the market had turned the other way, who knows if you two would still be friends.

DANA: Of course we'd still be friends. You don't throw away a 17 year-old friendship away over money.

ALEX: I'm just postulating.

DANA: *(Shooing ALEX off the subject.)* Postulate away. *(To KA-TIE.)* Do you think you'll be getting together with some of your Wall Street buds?

KATIE: I very well might.

DANA: Would you hit them up for some hot investment tips?

KATIE: You bet. I'm the one that needs help in that department. Major help.

DANA: Ever since you quit your job on Wall Street to write, I've been worried sick.

KATIE: Hey, you're not the only one.

DANA: Do you have anything to retire on? Josh have a good 401K? Life insurance?

KATIE: Oh, Dana.

DANA: Katie, this is important.

ALEX: You can't count on Social Security.

KATIE: I know. It's just that I'm tired, jetlagged –

DANA: Oh please. You have an MBA in Finance from the University of Chicago. Of all people, I know you can calculate the present and future value of money on the back of a cocktail napkin with your eyes closed.

KATIE: I appreciate your concern, truly, but I can't discuss this right now.

ALEX: Look, you two. There's a fascinating PBS documentary coming up next on capuchin monkeys. The female capuchins seem to have this notion of fairness and throw pebbles when there's a perceived injustice. Any interest? *(Short beat, no interest expressed.)* I didn't think so.

ALEX changes the channel on TV.

DANA: Katie, you can't depend on the arts. It's not wise.

KATIE: I know. Unfortunately I know.

DANA: That's why Alex and I buy so much. Someone has to support the arts. Why not us?

ALEX: Dana and I, we know art is a hard row. That's where we come in. Big buyers.

DANA: We love art. All kinds of art.

KATIE: I love the African masks on the wall.

ALEX: That window frame hails from Morocco. The pottery from Portugal. The rug, Tibetan.

KATIE: Who is that cute girl in the beaded frame?

DANA: We met that girl in Sri Lanka, on the beach. That girl offered us some pretty shells. We gave her twenty dollars. She gave us that million dollar smile.

KATIE: And that boy holding a snake?

DANA: We simply admired his fearlessness. To be eight and fearless. Can you imagine?

ALEX: Look at the art on this boy's tongue. We love to take photos of children on vacation. Gives us joy. They're our imaginary children.

KATIE: You have so much stuff. I barely own anything.

ALEX: Maybe Dana has a point, you shouldn't have left Wall Street.

DANA: We used to have more.

KATIE: More? Where would it fit?

DANA: Quite a few of our favorite valuables are missing thanks to Alex's crazy cousin Henry. Normal people steal electronics. Jewelry. Credit cards. Henry has a taste for the exotic, the less easily replaceable, the uninsured.

ALEX: Dana's philosophy is "Nature Abhors a Vacuum." If there's a space, fill it. Dana likes her nooks and crannies filled.

DANA: Would you trust someone who steals your Buddhas? That's like stealing your soul. Would you steal my soul?

ALEX: We're not Buddhists.

DANA: How do you know? We could be walking reincarnations.

ALEX: Cut Henry some slack, he grew up with nothing. Nothing.

DANA: So did I, but I don't steal.

ALEX: I guess you're better than him.

DANA: I am.

ALEX: I never liked those gold Buddhas anyway. I thought they were tacky as hell. Imagine, your 3 million dollar home resembling a greasy Thai restaurant. Tacky.

KATIE: Speaking of food, I'm starving. How does grabbing some dinner sound? My treat. Sorry, was that way rude?

DANA: Of course not. What are you in the mood for? Italian, Thai, Chinese --

KATIE: I wonder if this cozy little French bistro is still open for business. Where's your phone book?

DANA points.

ALEX: Wherever you guys go, you mind bringing me and Gigi back some food?

KATIE: Aren't you going to come with us?

ALEX: I don't want to rain on your parade. You two haven't seen each other in so long. Besides, this way you can drink. Just don't tell me. And use breath mints.

DANA: Please, Alex. Join us.

ALEX: What if my back starts acting up again? I'll just be in an embarrassing way.

DANA: Then take another painkiller. You promised.

ALEX: I know I did, dearest, but I'm staying in for us, saving myself up for Italy. I counted 23 confrontations today, roundtrip. Can you imagine 23 confrontations just to pick up your mail, some flowers, and a carton of juice? 23! Can you imagine? Between the energy and the confrontation, I ask you, where is life? I'm wiped.

KATIE: We can go somewhere very, very close. Or, take a taxi. So many delicious choices to tempt even the most discriminating palate.

DANA: I was so hoping my two dearest friends in the whole wide world would get a chance to know each other better.

ALEX: Sweetheart, I don't know about Katie, but I would love nothing more.

KATIE: Why don't we order in?

ALEX: Why don't we? We've only got a thousand menus.

DANA: You sure you don't mind?

KATIE: Plenty of time to eat out.

ALEX: We got all we need right here, including our darling irrepressible Gigi.

GIGI RESUMES VOCIFEROUS, OMINOUS BARKING.

SCENE 3

: *Morning of 9/11. Terrace off DANA and ALEX's Master Bedroom.*
AT RISE: The plane has just hit the first (North) Tower. DANA watches through binoculars. ALEX watches through a video camera. The LARGE TV in the master bedroom is on. CHAOS ensues.

DANA: Katie, get up! Get the fuck up! Katie!

KATIE stumbles up the stairs.

KATIE: Coming.

ALEX: Katie! Quick, or you'll miss everything!

KATIE: *(Muttering to herself.)* My god, don't they know it's still 5 AM in California?

DANA: Probably another Exxon Valdez. Pilot got drunk, or dropped acid, forgot to look where he was going.

ALEX: You think?

DANA: Got a better explanation?

ALEX: Stupid pilot. Don't we learn anything from our mistakes?

KATIE enters.

KATIE: What's wrong?

ALEX: A plane just hit one of the Twin Towers.

DANA: The North Tower.

KATIE: The Twin Towers? As in World Trade Center? *(Looking.)* Holy shit.

DANA: Wanna close-up?

DANA offers KATIE binoculars. Alex watches through the videocamera.

KATIE: How did this happen?

ALEX: We're thinking accident. Maybe the pilot fell asleep.

KATIE: Accident. What kind of accident?

ALEX: Not sure.

DANA: A stupid one.

ALEX: We were just trying to assess what level of stupidity.

KATIE: How'd you find out? Did you hear the crash?

ALEX: TV is the new god. I love TV.

DANA: Look at all the people on the rooftops. All over the city. Let's wave. "Good morning!"

KATIE: Jesus, I'm half-naked.

ALEX: Yeah, maybe you should grab some clothes.

DANA: Oh, Katie, I wouldn't worry about it, the City's attention is focused elsewhere at the moment.

KATIE: Still, I'd like to get a sweatshirt. I'm freezing. My high beams are flashing.

DANA: Alex, can't you loan her one of your shirts?

ALEX: Mine? What about yours?

DANA: Fine, Katie, go into our bedroom and grab whatever you want from my closet. Anything as long as you remember to return it.

KATIE: Of course I'd remember to return it.

DANA: I don't have time to explain and you don't have time to run downstairs. You might miss the best part.

KATIE: The best part?

DANA: You know, the moment when all the helicopters arrive, dump water on the building and save everyone. Wouldn't it be nice to start off the day heroically, with a happy ending?

SCENE 4

SETTING: Morning of 9/11. Terrace off DANA and ALEX's Master Bedroom.
AT RISE: ALEX, DANA and KATIE sit on the teak deck furniture, waiting for the helicopters. The large TV in the master bedroom is still on. ALEX continues to document the tragedy with his video camera. GIGI BARKS.

ALEX: Did you walk Gigi this morning?

DANA: I thought you were.

The second plane crashes into the South Tower. A BURST OF OR-ANGE.

DANA: Did you see that?

ALEX: I did. Got that second airplane on tape.

KATIE: What the hell is going on?

DANA: See what you would have missed if you went downstairs? If we didn't wake you?

ALEX: This no longer feels like an accident.

KATIE: It feels deliberate. Too deliberate.

ALEX: Oh my god, what are we going to do? What can we do?

DANA: I don't think we're going to Italy.

ALEX: No Italy? Oh my god, does this mean that we're trapped? How long? We can't just sit here and watch, can we?

DANA: What choice do we have, sweetie?

KATIE: There must be something we can do. Something proactive.

ALEX: Like what?

DANA: Well, like someone has to take Gigi for a walk and see what other people are doing. Maybe someone out there knows what to do.

ALEX: I think we should let her do her business on the terrace.

DANA: Alex, that's disgusting.

ALEX: When we toured Versailles, remember when I asked where the bathrooms were, what those stains were in the marble, remember how the tour guide told us that the people used to just lift up their dresses, drop their pants and shit and piss in the corner?

DANA: Can you be any less graphic?

KATIE: Is that true?

ALEX: *(Nods.)* What is a little dog doodoo compared to that?

DANA: You're cleaning it up.

ALEX: We should probably watch the news. Find out what the President is going to do, to protect us, to reassure us.

19

KATIE: Yes, let's find out what the media knows. What they advise us to do.

ALEX steps in, looks at the TV in the master bedroom.

ALEX: Shit. A plane also hit the Pentagon.

KATIE: The Pentagon too?

ALEX: According to CNN, there were 4 planes. One went down in Pennsylvania.

KATIE: What's going on? How many more planes are there?

ALEX: They say the fourth plane was headed for the nation's capital.

DANA: Holy shit, people are jumping to their deaths.

ALEX: Goddamnit! We're fucked. I've got to get a hold of my sponsor.

KATIE: Jumping?

DANA: Check it out.

DANA offers KATIE her binoculars.

KATIE: No thanks. I can see fine where I am. My view is plenty unobstructed.

DANA: Isn't that where you used to work?

KATIE: Yes.

DANA: You might know some of these people.

KATIE: *(Takes the binoculars for a second, then hands them back.)* I can't, I'm too frightened. I need the hope.

ALEX: Katie, you have friends up there? In there? How many?

DANA: God knows how many.

KATIE: Many. Too many.

ALEX: Great. Fucking great. Where's the joy of being stone cold sober if you can't shut out the pain?

KATIE: When I traded, we worked with Cantor Fitzgerald every day. Used to visit my brokers Vic and Ray on the 105th floor. The building shakes. Even on a clear day.

DANA: We used to sip champagne and watch the sunset at Windows on the World.

KATIE: There are a lot of companies at the World Trade Center. Thousands of employees.

ALEX: Thousands! Oh my god, how are they all going to get out? This is too upsetting. They can't all get out, can they?

KATIE: I don't know. *(Trying to convince herself.)* But miracles happen every day, right?

DANA: We're on the 10th floor and I don't think we'd survive if we jumped.

ALEX: I think we should move. Live on the ground floor. It'd be better for my back. Of course, the value of this penthouse has probably just dropped astronomically now that we can't say we have a stunning view of the Twin Towers. Oh my god, what am I saying, how are those people going to get out?

KATIE: Alex, please we can't give up hope so fast.

DANA: Why don't we pray?

ALEX: To whom?

KATIE: God?

DANA: Buddha?

ALEX: *(Clasping his hands together in prayer.)* To Whom It May Concern, please save our godforsaken asses. Please don't let us down. Please numb our pain and wipe away our fears. Until then, I'm going to help myself to some Valium. The pain is too sharp. Amen.

DANA: What are you going to do?

KATIE: What would you do? What can I do?

DANA: Tell me about some of these people.

KATIE: Ray took me to Petrossian for my 25th. We ate so much caviar, stuffed ourselves to the gills. Vic loves to cook. He's single, lives alone, but he goes to the trouble to cook these elaborate gourmet meals for himself. Just for one. How many people do you know would take the time? I was going to call them and see if they wanted to meet for lunch, or cook together.

DANA: Go on. Tell me more.

KATIE: I can't breathe. The clouds of past tense closing in, I can't breathe.

DANA: I think you should start assembling a list of all the people you know that could be in those buildings.

KATIE: And start making some phone calls.

DANA: Yes. I'll help.

KATIE: Maybe some of them changed jobs and neglected to tell me.

DANA: You switched careers.

KATIE: Maybe some of them are on vacation.

DANA: We were headed to Italy.

KATIE: Maybe some of them called in sick.

DANA: There is still hope. Wisps of hope.

ALEX: I've brought reinforcements. Box of tissues. Water. Cold compresses. Valium.

KATIE: I can't give up hope at the speed of gravity times mass.

DANA: You better call Josh. Let him know what's going on. Beg him to stay home.

KATIE: You think something bad will happen in L.A?

DANA: Just in case.

ALEX: You never know. Not after today.

KATIE: Do our phones work?

ALEX grabs the cordless.

ALEX: Miracle number one. A dial tone.

KATIE: I hate to wake Josh up. It's still so early in California. He barely gets enough sleep.

DANA: Does Josh work in a tall building? Tall enough to attract unwanted attention?

KATIE: Only the second tallest building west of the Mississippi. *(Realizing.)* Give me the phone.

22

ALEX hands KATIE the phone.

ALEX: He's going to be so glad you called.

KATIE: *(Dials.)* Josh?

LIGHTS FADE. ALEX, DANA and KATIE sit in the teak chairs, using cold compresses and emptying boxes of tissue. SPOTLIGHT on TV showing the FALL of the TWIN TOWERS. BLACKOUT.

SCENE 5

SETTING: DANA and ALEX's living room.
AT RISE: The huge TV is still on, CNN. Suitcases packed for Italy stand near the door. The phone RINGS nonstop in the penthouse.

ALEX: I can't fucking believe the twin towers collapsed.

DANA: Who can?

ALEX: I thought America was strong. Invincible.

DANA: We all did. Honey, you're pacing.

ALEX: How come everybody's phone is down, but ours? How did we get chosen as Grand Central Station? It's for you again, Katie. How is it you know so many people? What are you, a social butterfly? I'm beginning to feel as if Dana and I don't know anyone.

KATIE: Sorry. I told all these people I was going to be in New York City for three weeks so I gave them your phone number. I thought it'd be okay.

DANA: Alex, it's not Katie's fault.

ALEX: Of course not. Sorry, Katie. I'm just annoyed because I was counting on Italy. I needed Italy. The Romance. The Fresh Air. The Art.

KATIE: I understand. We're all rattled.

KATIE goes off to talk privately.

DANA: Hey, you're not the only one hurting. I was looking forward to practicing my Italian. *Prego. Belissimo. Basta.*

ALEX: When do you think the airports going to open up? I want the first flight after that.

DANA: Are you nuts? I'm not getting on any plane.

23

ALEX: Don't you feel ambushed? We have to fight back.

DANA: Honey, I'm not sure I'm ready to fly again. If ever.

ALEX: Then let's rent a car. Drive as far away as we can. Find some beauty. North Carolina. Arkansas. Tennessee. Let's get the hell away from all this ugliness and these awful carcinogenic smells.

DANA: You heard the news. The bridges and tunnels are closed.

ALEX: *(Grabs a Kleenex.)* Goddamnit! It isn't fair. It isn't fucking fair. I need a vacation. And the day we can finally get away, the FAA shuts down the airports nationwide. For the first time in history. We're trapped. The terrorists have won.

DANA: At least we're alive. Think of all those people. We're the lucky ones.

ALEX: I don't feel much like a survivor.

DANA : Those poor people. All gone in one fell swoop. Poor Katie, has to try and figure out where everyone is, was. Isn't she great, the way she's able to take charge?

ALEX: I haven't been able to reach my sponsor. Where is he?

DANA: Oh dear.

ALEX: What if?

DANA: No. Keep trying.

KATIE hangs up the phone.

KATIE: Alex. Dana. Some of my friends are stuck in the City. They can't get home. I was wondering and they were wondering if they could come here, just until the City opens back up, until they can get home. Safely. If it'd be OK since you have so much room.

DANA: Sure –

ALEX: Sure?

DANA: It'd be our pleasure.

ALEX: Shouldn't we ask how many friends? Who these people are?

KATIE: Totally fair question. Tori is a sculptor, met her at an artist colony. Roy and I used to work on Wall Street together. Chris was my neighbor when I lived in East Village, works in the public library, a regular sweet guy. Mark is a fellow writer, we used to belong to the same writers group. Hervé is a jazz musician, plays saxophone.

24

DANA: Alex. This is our chance to be useful. To make a difference. Meet interesting new people.

ALEX: Can't we just write a check like we usually do? I'm not sure I'm ready to meet new people. I'm not in any state to be social. I feel so vulnerable. At my worst.

KATIE: You don't have to be social, I promise.

ALEX: I don't? But that doesn't seem quite right.

DANA: Katie's right, in times like these, nobody expects anyone to be hostess with the mostest.

KATIE: I wouldn't ask, but they don't have anywhere to go and they're my friends. Good people. Just like you and me. I swear.

ALEX: I feel like I'm going to fall apart. Just like those Towers. Without any warning. Where the fuck is President Bush?

DANA: Alex, we have plenty of food and room. I stocked up for Katie's visit. I think it could be good for us, to grieve together, hold hands, form our own support group. Couldn't your back use a little more support?

ALEX: I'm not used to breaking down in front of strangers. Total strangers.

DANA: Who is?

KATIE: You'll be among friends.

ALEX: Is that dog shit I smell?

DANA: How can you distinguish anything from that overpowering stench of charred human flesh?

KATIE: It reeks, doesn't it? And the dust --

ALEX: Did anyone take poor Gigi out for a walk?

KATIE: I'll take Gigi out for a walk if you'll let my friends crash here temporarily.

DANA: If that's not a bargain, Alex –

KATIE: Please I have to do something. Help in some small way. It's the only thing that keeps me going. Knowing there's something I can do.

DANA: I'm going to donate supplies, on behalf of both us, Alex.

ALEX: No one's going to make fun of me if I stay in bed all day, or burst into tears at the drop of a hat.

KATIE: Of course not.

ALEX: Oh, all right. But soon as it's safe, your friends are outta here.

DANA: *(Hugs and pecks ALEX.)* Thanks, honeybunch. I'm so proud to be your wife.

KATIE: Thanks, Alex. You're a peach.

ALEX: Peaches bruise easily, you know.

KATIE: *(Complimenting ALEX.)* They also have strong pits. That hold firm, even under duress.

DANA: Hear that, Alex? Katie just paid you a compliment.

ALEX: Where do you get your energy? Your bounce?

KATIE: I'm not quite sure.

ALEX: Do you take vitamins? Work out? Cocaine?

KATIE: Cocaine? You think I'm a cokehead?

DANA: When we were in high school, Katie used to be an insomniac.

KATIE: Used to? I still am.

ALEX: What do you have against sleep?

KATIE: I wish I could sleep through the night. I wish I could sleep well. Regularly. I certainly want to. But I've always been a light sleeper. Things keep me awake. All sorts of things. Stupid things, little things, big things. Some days I feel so completely exhausted –

ALEX: *(Totally relating.)* You feel you could snap in two.

KATIE: *(Same wavelength.)* Yes.

ALEX: That's me most days.

DANA: Have you tried drinking herbal tea half an hour before going to bed?

KATIE: Problem with tea is you have to wake up in the middle of the night to pee.

ALEX: Would you like a Valium? I have plenty.

KATIE: No. No thank you.

ALEX: Why not? It works. It really numbs the pain so you can rest. Finally rest.

KATIE: As idiotic as it sounds, I've grown afraid of the dark. I want to be awake. I crave the light.

ALEX: You're strange. Strange in a good way.

KATIE: Thanks. I better go call my friends and tell them it's OK for them to crash here.

KATIE disappears with the phone.

ALEX: Where is all this dust coming from? You don't think they're human remains, it's bad enough inhaling the dead, but to also be sitting in it and seeing the dust collect everywhere --

DANA: No. Stop. Please don't worry about the dust. Dust can be swept up, away, out. I'll take care of it. Later. I promise.

ALEX: *(Teasing.)* Dana the dust buster. That's not the Dana I know and love.

DANA: Have I told you lately how proud I am of you?

ALEX: For what? I feel so weak.

DANA: I'm proud of you for expanding your heart, for being kind and generous and strong –

ALEX: *(Teasing.)* Is that all?

DANA: For beating alcohol. Substance abuse.

ALEX: It ain't over until it's over.

DANA: We're gonna make it through this. Together. I'm sure of it.

ALEX: Oh, Dana, that's why I love you so much. You're always so sure. So positively sure. I wish I could be so sure. Sure and steady.

SCENE 6

SETTING: DANA and ALEX's living room now functions as a crisis support center, filled with people in various states of distress, undress and grief. TV continues to drone on.
AT RISE: ALEX still controls the TiVo remote and channel surfs. Katie's friends MARK, TORI, CHRIS, HERVÉ settle in. KATIE is in charge of a long list of names on a bulletin board, tracking who's been reached (safe) and who's "missing." DANA serves liquid refreshments. CHRIS lights lavender-scented candles. Everyone takes turns using the phone to call people.

CHRIS: Everybody inhale. Take deep breaths.

EVERYONE COUGHS from the fumes and dust.

ALEX: *(Covering his nose.)* Are you nuts? I bet the noxious fumes alone shave five years off our lives.

DANA: Five whole years?

ALEX: We need more duct tape.

CHRIS: Lavender is supposed to be very soothing.

MARK: Let's meditate. Or, chant.

TORI: I don't know if I have an apartment anymore.

DANA: There, there. At least you're alive. Count your blessings.

TORI: Everything I owned could fit in your kitchen.

DANA: Then you didn't lose very much, did you?

TORI: You trying to make me feel better?

DANA: Every cloud has a silver lining, Tori. Sometimes you have to really look for it.

CHRIS: Shit, man, this guy's saying this terrorist attack is directly related to the bombing in 1993. Have we been asleep at the wheel? That fuckface is saying it's our fault. We were warned. Warned, my ass.

CHRIS grabs onto ALEX, tightly.

CHRIS: Were we warned? Is it our fault? Did we do this to ourselves?

ALEX: Please, the very idea that we asked for it, it's too much to bear.

CHRIS: I'll say. What's the world coming to when we blame the victim?

MARK: Are you saying we're all innocent? Completely innocent?

CHRIS: Apparently you're not.

TORI: Something to confess?

CHRIS: Out with it. You know something about those terrorists?

KATIE: Hey, Mark writes books.

CHRIS: What kind of books? Anti-American books?

MARK: I don't owe you any explanations.

ALEX: Please, everyone, I'm not well.

DANA: It's his back.

HERVÉ: Perhaps now is the perfect time for a group hug.

ALEX: Group hug? What will that accomplish?

HERVÉ: You prefer a more personalized hug, Alex? One that fits the curvature of your spine?

DANA: I believe that's my job.

ALEX: Where is Gigi? Has anyone seen Gigi?

MARK: Who's Gigi?

ALEX: Our darling Westie.

MARK: Oh. That thing.

TORI: I'm not much of a dog person either.

ALEX: Please dear god, don't tell me someone let her out by mistake. The smoke alone could kill her.

CHRIS: She could be anywhere. This place is huge.

HERVÉ: You want me to help you look for Gigi?

DANA: Please, if everyone could stop what they're doing and –

KATIE: She's hiding behind the drapes.

DANA: What's she doing there? I hope she's not ingesting all that toxic dust.

ALEX: What a relief, Gigi's okay. I almost had a heart attack.

HERVÉ: Time for a big bear bug.

ALEX: Well...

HERVÉ: I insist.

HERVÉ hugs ALEX tight, massaging his back.

HERVÉ: That wasn't so bad, was it?

ALEX: You think you could massage my back some more?

HERVÉ: *Absolument.*

HERVÉ kneads ALEX's back.

HERVÉ: Hey, Alex, where are your souvenirs from France?

DANA: Stolen.

HERVÉ: *Quel dommage.* Pity.

DANA: Isn't it?

HERVÉ: Just gives you another excuse to return to France. If you like, I could show you around.

ALEX: I love France.

HERVÉ: Who doesn't?

DANA: You love France? Since when?

ALEX: Since we visited.

Doorbell RINGS.

MARK: I'll get the door. It's probably my friend Dominick.

It's ROY. Mark is visibly disappointed.

ROY: Hi, I'm Roy. Katie's friend.

MARK: Come on in.

ROY: Don't look so disappointed.

MARK: Sorry, it's just that I was expecting, hoping you were going to be Dominick.

ROY: How long has he been missing?

MARK: 48 hours.

ROY: Oh dear. Was he on a high floor?

MARK: 95th.

ROY: Poor, poor Dominick.

DANA: I'm so sorry, Mark. Let me refresh your drink.

MARK: You think? No. Not Dominick.

CHRIS: He refuses to face facts.

MARK: People, please, let's not jump to dismal conclusions before we have to.

HERVÉ: Let us light some more candles and say a prayer for Mark's bon ami Dominick.

ROY: Where's Katie? I have to talk to her.

DANA: In the kitchen. Cooking. She'll be out shortly. Hi, I'm Dana.

ROY: Roy.

ALEX: What on earth were your parents thinking when they named you Roy?

ROY: They weren't. Parents named me Helen which I changed to Roy.

ALEX: And why would any woman want to be called Roy?

ROY: I'm not any woman.

ALEX: 'Course not, that would be too fucking easy.

ROY: How do you and Katie know each other?

DANA: Roy, this is my husband Alex. Katie and I were best friends in high school.

CHRIS: That's so touching. Remarkable.

MARK: High school? Gross. I don't keep in touch with anyone from high school.

TORI: Me neither.

ROY: Seriously. High school is so over.

KATIE: *(Teasing.)* You're just jealous.

KATIE returns with a steaming bowl of pasta.

KATIE: Pasta's ready if you are. But please, nobody force feed themselves. Eat only if you can.

DANA: Lucky I stocked the refrigerator. I even have some freshly grated Parmesan Reggiano.

HERVÉ: *Mangez!* We must replenish what we have lost.

ALEX: What if we've lost too much?

ROY: Katie.

KATIE: I'm so glad you're safe.   I was worried sick.

ROY: I'm alive because I was laid off.

KATIE: Laid off. Since when? Why didn't you tell me?

ROY: It's been over a year. Almost two.

KATIE: So what? You should have told me.

ROY: The good news is I found Susan. She was hung-over so didn't show up for work.

MARK: Who wants to use the phone next?

HERVÉ: *Moi, s'il vous plait.*

TORI: Is it my turn yet? I need to call my therapist.

ALEX: If you don't mind, I'd like to give my friend another try.

TORI: Of course, it is your phone.

CHRIS: Do I smell dog shit?

MARK: Somebody needs to clean up around here.

ROY: The bad news is….Connor's missing.

KATIE: Why you telling me?

ROY: I thought you'd want to know.

KATIE: I don't.

ROY: You two were so close. You knew him so well.

KATIE: Once. Or so I thought.

ROY: Connor was there, Katie. I know it. I was just there last week.

KATIE: Last week. You kept in touch with him? After what he did to me?

ROY: I had to. I'm unemployed I thought he could help me find work.

KATIE: And he didn't, did he? Didn't think so.

ROY: What if he, you know –

KATIE: Went up in flames?

ROY: I knew you'd care. In spite of everything.

KATIE: No. He always had a way out. An escape route.

DANA: How does all this dust get in and settle here? Layers and layers of dust. I hope this isn't getting into our lungs. How you doing, Alex?

ALEX: I'm on permahold with Air Italia.

DANA: I thought you were trying to get a hold of you-know-who.

ALEX: I was. No answer.

DANA: Any luck?

ALEX: None. Now, I'm trying to get through to the airlines. We are going to Italy. One way or another. We got to get out of here. Soon as possible.

DANA: Sweetheart, Giuliani asked all New Yorkers to stay home. To stay put.

ALEX: I hate staying put. Who's in fucking charge here?

TORI: *(Overlapping.)* Who knows?

CHRIS: *(Overlapping.)* Dick Cheney.

MARK: *(Overlapping.)* No one.

ALEX: Damn it, that settles it, I'm calling the White House.

DANA: The White House?

ALEX: I demand to speak to someone of authority.

CHRIS: You can't just call the President of the United States.

ALEX: Why not? Are we not concerned American citizens? Taxed to the wazoo?!

MARK: Don't you think the President's a little busy?

ALEX: Too busy for his fellow Americans?

ROY: Yeah, like Bush is going to talk to you.

ALEX: Like the President wants to talk to a girl named Roy and a boy named Sue.

KATIE: Alex is right.

ALEX: *(Surprised.)* I am?

KATIE: Why can't we call the President? Are we not worthy?

ROY: Can you call someone you didn't elect?

KATIE: Very least, it'll make us feel better. Like we're doing something. Something vital. Worse comes to worse, we tried.

HERVÉ: Do you know what you are going to say?

ALEX: I have questions.

DANA: We all have questions.

Questions are fired quickly and overlap.

ALEX: *(Overlapping.)* Where the hell you been, George "Dubya?"

DANA: *(Overlapping.)* Where are you when we need you?

MARK: *(Overlapping.)* How could you just sit there, reading after you knew?

TORI: *(Overlapping.)* What were you thinking?

ROY: *(Overlapping.)* Were you thinking?

CHRIS: *(Overlapping.)* Do people hate us, or do they hate you?

KATIE: *(Overlapping.)* Are you going to kill the people who killed my friends and former colleagues, or not?

KATIE covers her mouth, surprised at her strong outburst.

DANA: Put it on speaker phone.

ALEX: We need leadership. Lead us, George "Dubya," lead us to the promised land, flash us a beacon of hope.

BUSY TONE. ALEX hits redial. BUSY TONE. Redial. BUSY TONE. Short, sullen beat.

ALEX: We're all fucked.

ALEX turns off the speakerphone. Suddenly BUSH appears on TV.

GEORGE "DUBYA" BUSH: *(Via TV.)* My fellow Americans. Do not worry. Do not panic. I am with you. Aboard Air Force One. Protecting you from an undisclosed location. But even aboard this safe, enclosed space, I assure you we will not let these acts of terrorism go unpunished. This will not stand. We will get Osama Bin Laden. Dead, or alive. We will smoke them out. We will get these evil-doers. I've directed resources. The search is underway. For those of you who speak English, we are going to kick some motherfucking ass. Meanwhile, I'd like to ask each and every one of you a favor. Pray. Donate. Buy. That's right, go out and buy something. Afraid to leave your house to shop. Got one word for you: Internet. Buy something substantial. Charge it. Pay cash. Borrow. Doesn't matter how you pay for it. What matters is your commitment. Do it for one of our fallen heroes. Do it for the failing economy. Just do it. Conspicuous consumption is the best revenge.

DANA: So that's why he couldn't answer the phone. It's not that he doesn't care, he was about to broadcast live.

ALEX: God bless America.

ROY: Does anyone here feel better? Feel much like shopping?

TORI: With whose money?

DANA: Mine.

TORI: Serious?

DANA: It's my patriotic duty. Plus, we'll have fun. Loads of fun. And on that note, who could use a refill?

ROY: God could I use another potent potable.

EVERYONE except ALEX raises their glass. Suspicious, ALEX heads to the grandfather clock, opens it to discover vodka bottles stashed inside.

ALEX: Goddamnit. Are you guys drinking water, or vodka?

Short beat. No answer. ALEX walks over to inspect people's drinks.

ALEX: Is that sparkling water, or sparkling wine? Goddamnit! Everybody out!

TORI: Out?

DANA: Alex sweetheart, it's my fault, I told them you couldn't drink, that you were in A.A., but I thought it wouldn't hurt you if you didn't know. I'm sorry.

ROY: We're trying to drown out that pungent smell of molten steel and searing human flesh.

KATIE: Alex, please, have some compassion. It won't happen again. We promise.

ALEX: Compassion.

DANA: We can't even open the windows. It's so stifling.

MARK: Grocery stores are out of fresh produce.

CHRIS: I saw a looter stab another looter in the chest. All that blood for a fake Rolex.

HERVÉ: Blame me. You know the French, we can't live without our wine.

ALEX: I know our penthouse seems posh, but in case you haven't noticed, the spaces are jam-packed.

TORI: But where will we go if you kick us out? I'm homeless.

ALEX: My back feels like it's going to crumble, and my poor Gigi's coughing up a lung, but is anyone showing me compassion?

DANA: Of course we are. We all are.

HERVÉ: Come here, let me give you another hug.

DANA: Group hug.

ALEX: I can't get a hold of my sponsor. I can't hold my back up against the world.

SCENE 7

SETTING: DANA and ALEX's living room.
AT RISE: SUSAN emerges from the large TV screen, sharing her tale of survival.

SUSAN: I fell off the water wagon night before 9/11. I didn't want to, but I ran into Bobby. My ex. Bobby and I were word-processing at this biotech firm at World Trade Center. I ran into him at Gristedes the night before, he's looking really hot, groping the juicy vine ripe tomatoes. He's trying to switch labels, see if he can fool the cashier so he can pay $1.99 per pound instead of $3.99. Bobby offers to make me farfalle with tomato concasse, yellow squash and soft shell crab. The problem with exes, they know your weak points and go for the kill. I was all defiant and stiff, yeah yeah, nice, whatever, until Bobby said Susan, soft shell crab. Then I melted down like nutty brown butter. On one condition, I said. I can't drink. No alcohol. Take it or leave it.

We used to drink like a fish, Bobby and me. Over dinner, Bobby asks me who or what gave me the crazy idea that I am an alcoholic. Don't we drink to live? To survive? Bobby, please don't tell me you think our drinking days were healthy.

Remember what I said about exes knowing where you hurt most. Bobby sharpened those knives and wasted no time sticking them in. How else we gonna stomach our shitty day jobs? Handle the pressure and tension of the precarious art world? Handling the nerves that shatter when we open that impersonal rejection letter. When your mom says, I like the paintings you did in high school the best. Isn't alcohol more like motor oil, the lubricant that keeps the giant machine running, breathing? Humming along smoothly, enabling us to stomach the indigestible questions of when you gonna get a real job, whatcha gonna do when you're old, you gonna rent all your fucking life?

But, Bobby, I ask, trying real hard to resist, I can't stand it when I blackout. I can't stand waking up in the morning with these black and blue marks, not knowing how I got 'em. I'm embarrassed when I wake up in the morning, bound up with some man like a human pretzel, and I gotta ask him his name, if we had sex, if he used a condom. Bobby, he thwacked my head and said, Susan, who you been fucking behind my back? Oh god, Bobby, my eyes are welling up, was it all just a drunken stupor? I thought we broke up. Bobby tweaks my breast and says, just tuning your radio, girl. Tuning your radio.

SUSAN (cont.): I like your FM. Don't you see, some people would give their left nut to forget, to start over. That's what alcohol does for me. I get to erase the past and start fucking over. I can't hear the sound of other voices nagging. Every day is a new day. Brand new. No clouds. Clear skies.

Until Bobby said that, I never looked at alcohol as my Echinacea. My salvation. That is, until I couldn't show up to work the next day because me and Bobby were so hung-over and entwined, we didn't hear the alarm. Bobby and me are together again. Drinking. Enjoying every fifth. Fuck A.A. Hello, my name's Susan and I'm an alcoholic. Alcohol saved my life.

SCENE 8

SETTING: DANA and ALEX's living room.
AT RISE: 21 YEAR OLD emerges from the large TV screen, sharing his/her tale of survival.

21 YEAR OLD: Today was supposed to be my 21st birthday. I say supposed to because how could I possibly celebrate? I had been looking forward to this date for years. My friends planned to surprise me with a wild birthday bash – kegs of beer, strippers, fireworks. My wild party plans were blown to smithereens, my birthday fell apart with the collapse of hope and life. Turning 21 was supposed to be a defining moment. A day to remember. A day I'd get to look back and say, damn, those were the good ole days. My crazy carefree salad days. The days I danced atop bar tables, ran naked through water fountains, and clumsily swung for the stars. The days I embraced life with reckless abandon and lusty *joie de vivre*. Now I can't help but wonder, will I ever be allowed the privilege of enjoying my birthday again? Of being happy and silly on September 11th? Or will the day I was born always be the day too many people died? I want to feel my age, an age of promise, of multiple choice. You can't reverse time, you only turn 21 once. But instead of feeling 21, I feel 50 something. Like my life is half over. I've been robbed.

SCENE 9

SETTING: New York and Atlanta. NYC: Dark of night, guest room where KATIE is staying. Atlanta: A private study.
AT RISE: SIRENS blare. Phone RINGS. KATIE picks up the phone right away to avoid disturbing the others and soon as she picks up, LIGHTS UP on PROFESSOR MADDEN in Atlanta.

PROFESSOR MADDEN: Katie Fields? I know it's the middle of the night, but I can't sleep. I really need your help. No, we've never actually met, but you dated my son. My son Connor. Connor Madden.

Oh, I know it's been a long time, and it must seem like another lifetime ago to you, but my Connor, he used to talk a lot about you. He nursed high hopes that you were the one. You really energized him. You were his idol. He used to carry a picture of you in his wallet. The photo of you in his red Porsche. Remember that? I'm staring at a copy of that photo right now.

The reason I'm calling is, we haven't heard from our son. We can't get through to anyone who knows him. My wife, she automatically thinks the worst, but me, I know better. I know Connor is alive. Now, I'd come up there myself, drive all night from Atlanta if I have to, to prove to the Missus she's wrong, except, as you know, all the airports have been shut down, the bridges and tunnels. Access to Manhattan is blocked. I need you, Katie, to look for Connor. Find him, let us know he's safe. Will you do that for me, honey?

I did try his firm, but I couldn't get through. Unfortunately, I don't know any of his friends, or his other colleagues. I know you two broke up, but surely whatever it was that caused you two to split must seem incredibly trivial in light of this world tragedy. You didn't keep in touch? No? How odd. In our last conversation, Connor told us he still loves you.

Connor sent us your two-page profile in the *New York Times* last year – congratulations, by the way, we liked your cowboy boots -- how you said you gave up trading bonds on Wall Street because you wanted to follow your heart. That's all I'm asking you to do. Listen.

PROFESSOR MADDEN places the phone across his chest so Katie can hear it beating.

Please, Katie. Listen to my beating heart. Connor loves you. Therefore, I love you too.

PROFESSOR MADDEN hangs up. We hear the DIALTONE. BLACKOUT. Then KATIE turns on a light. LIGHTS UP on KATIE as she grabs the phone and paces.

KATIE: *(Trembling)* Josh. My mentor from my Wall Street days is missing. His father begged me to look for him. Pulled out all the stops. Fanciful stops. Then claims I'm his last hope. Ironic, huh? It's killing me. Why does this have to fall on my head?

KATIE (cont.): Do I have to? Do you think if I said no, I could live with myself? Could you? What do I owe this man? This man who "inspired" me to leave Wall Street. Yeah, that guy. Him. If I refuse, how am I going to explain why to his desperate father? Are we ever allowed to speak ill of those who might be dead? Even when they deserve it? Or, does unforgivable tragedy wash away our past sins and therefore, I should let his father believe whatever he wants to believe, no matter how outlandish and outrageous. And if he's dead, God help me, is it in any way my fault? Could I have somehow prevented it?

SCENE 10

SETTING: ALEX and DANA's living room.
AT RISE: CHRIS delivers a monologue.

CHRIS: I don't understand. Why do they hate us? Why are some people saying we brought this tragedy onto ourselves? What did we do to piss off the world? What could we have done to deserve such monumental retaliation?

It's true, I suck at world geography, speak only one language and I've only been out of the country once. To England. But it's not like I don't want to see the world. I would love to travel more. Master a foreign language. Meet new people, see how others live. Open my eyes, expand my horizons. But in America, we barely get any vacation. I hardly make ends meet. You heard right, I'm a working stiff, I live hand to mouth.

This penthouse is not mine. Most people do not live like this. No idea if Alex and Dana are richer than they deserve to be. To me, that question is as futile as asking why is half the oil in the Middle East? The diamonds in Africa? The disparity between richer and poorer is devastating here too. Most of us have no real say, no control – in spite of all our protests and petitions – no control over what troops get sent where, where the market will close tomorrow, who our next President will be. C'mon, you saw what happened in Florida, the nation voted for Gore, but Bush stands unilaterally in power. Exceptions rule.

SCENE 11

SETTING: ALEX and DANA's living room. On large screen TV, the Oklahoma Bombing Memorial is projected.
AT RISE: OKLAHOMA BOMBING SURVIVOR emerges from the large TV to deliver her monologue.

OKLAHOMA BOMBING SURVIVOR: I love New York. New York is where I found myself. Where I fell in love. Dan and I used to see all the shows. Sip cappuccino in Little Italy, dim sum in Chinatown, Summerstage in Central Park. New York was our adult Disneyland. We couldn't get enough of New York, of each other, so we tied the knot. Got married at the South Street Seaport with the Brooklyn Bridge lighting up the heavens. When we decided to have children, Dan and I thought maybe it was time to move somewhere where there'd be more space. More grass. More balance. Somewhere we could be normal. Safe. Somewhere we could afford day care.

Dan and I was dropping Zack and Janey off at day care when an explosion ripped through the Alfred P. Murrah Federal Building, blowing them to smithereens. It was the worst terrorist attack on U.S. soil. April 19, 1995. 9:02 AM. The blast could be felt over 15 miles away. 168 victims killed. 500 people injured. Countless others lost friends and relatives. How was this loss memorialized? A wall with a reflecting pool. Small, empty chairs. Nine rows of chairs to represent the nine floors of the building. Chairs composed of bronze, stone and glass. With the largest concentration of chairs in the center where the main impact of the bomb was greatest.

The memorial is beautiful, sad and now a stark reminder that Okies are worth much less than New Yorkers. Minimum a million dollars less. Where's my act of Congress? My trash bags filled with cold cash? Where's my check, Mr. Feinberg? I lost 3 people, Mr. Feinberg. My entire family, my *raison d'être*. Why am I less worthy of sympathy and compensation? It's not about the money. It's about respect. It's about that gaping hole in my heart, the bottomless pit of loss. The rubble of grief that gives beneath your feet and threatens to swallow you whole. Don't turn away because you think I'm bitter and unconsolable. Turn away because you know as well as I do that no matter where you are, where you choose to live, raise a family, you are not safe and there's not a goddamned thing you can do about it.

<u>END OF ACT ONE</u>

ACT TWO

THE SEARCH FOR HUMAN REMAINS

SCENE 1

SETTING: Union Square, New York City. Thousands of posters and photos. Candles and flowers strewn everywhere.
AT RISE: KATIE and DANA post CONNOR's photo and information. MOURNERS mill about, posting and grieving.

DANA: Missing. Jim, AKA Jimbo Sherman, was just starting his first day at Windows on the World. First day.

KATIE: Oh my god, first day.

DANA: 25 years old.

KATIE: How tragic.

DANA: Isn't it?

KATIE: Mercedes Salvador, janitorial services, single mother of 4, lived in Jackson Heights

DANA: Four? No husband? No father for the kids? Those poor children.

KATIE: Says here Mercedes sent money home regularly to her parents. Maybe her parents will take in the kids.

DANA: So many people. So many of them so young. Prime of life.

KATIE: I know. When do the tears stop?

DANA: So many, too many, too sad.

KATIE: Unfulfilled broken promises.   I feel like an entire nation has died.

DANA: How can I absorb all these stories?   We could cry all day, all night and still it would not be enough.   How are we supposed to go on?

KATIE: What choice do we have?

DANA: Suddenly I feel very American and I want to buy a flag. A very large American flag. Express my patriotism.

KATIE: Yeah? Go for it.

DANA: I want to stare at those stars and stripes and contemplate what it means to be an American.

KATIE: You'll let me know when you know?

DANA looks closely at one of the posters.

DANA: Oh my god, suddenly I feel like I'm drowning in this bottomless pit of tears. I can't swim. I can't get to shore.

KATIE: What's wrong?

DANA: That looks a lot like Alex's cousin Henry except --

KATIE: The one who stole your Buddha?

DANA: Except Cousin Henry is a bum, a party animal, he couldn't have been down there. What reason would Cousin Henry have to be down there so early in the morning?

KATIE: It says here that Henry was last seen wearing this dress on 9/11. Stylish dress. Is that why you call him crazy cousin Henry? Because crazy cousin Henry is a transvestite with splashy tastes?

DANA: I don't feel so well. It's too overwhelming.

KATIE: I'll walk you home.

DANA: No.

KATIE: No? Are you sure?

DANA: You have more important things to do.

KATIE: I'm almost finished here.

DANA: I have to go buy something. It's the least I can do, for the failing economy. Shop. I'm afraid I'm not very good at much else.

KATIE: Dana, what are you talking about? You're talking nonsense. You are so generous. Thoughtful. Giving.

DANA: If you get home before I do, tell Alex I went to donate blood.

KATIE: You can't donate blood when you look like you're about to keel over. I won't let you.

DANA: Then I'll buy more supplies. Feed some firemen. Anything. Something other than sink.

KATIE: What's wrong? Talk to me.

DANA: I can't stay here.

KATIE: Then let's get out of here.

DANA: I'm sorry I can't go with you, to help you find that guy. I know I promised.

KATIE: Don't worry about it.

DANA: I feel like I know all these people. It's too much. I feel sick. Damaged.

KATIE: Let me help you locate crazy cousin Henry. Given what you've said, it's very likely he's nursing a hangover in someone else's bed. So the sooner we find Henry, the better.

KATIE pulls down the poster of HENRY and hands it to DANA.

DANA: No. You have enough on your shoulders.

KATIE: What's one more? What are friends for?

DANA: Katie, how could I be so oblivious? So fucking oblivious?

KATIE: What are you talking about?

DANA: This man that resembles Cousin Henry, he's wearing my dress. A dress I've been missing for months.

KATIE: Maybe it's just a coincidence.

DANA: That's what I want to believe, but what if it isn't? What does it say about me? And Alex? Katie, why does my world feel like it's caving in?

KATIE: Here, let's find you a cab. You need to go home and rest.

DANA: I can't. Every time I look out the window....the view, the view just isn't interesting or inspiring any more. Now every time I look out the window, I'm see smoke and holes and death – Terror.

KATIE: I know. We're all hurting.

DANA: Alex is right. Too much pain in the world. It's too much. We've got to get away before it's too late.

SCENE 2

SETTING: *Farmers Market. Union Square.*
AT RISE: *VENDORS selling their wares.*

VENDOR: Freedom fries, freedom fries. Fresh out of the fryer. Get your freedom fries. Hot and crunchy. Freedom fries.

VENDOR 2: Freedom toast. Freedom toast. Get your freedom toast with patriotic Vermont maple syrup. Freedom toast.

VENDOR 3: Freedom flags, freedom flags.

HERVÉ enters, wanders the market place.

HERVÉ: Toast? What are we toasting?

VENDOR 3: Freedom. Want a freedom flag? Goes well in any window. One size fits all.

VENDOR: Live free or die.

HERVÉ: To Freedom. I was wondering, have any of you seen Betty? I bought heirloom tomatoes from Betty a few days ago, down at the world trade center, but soon as the plane hit, everyone scrammed. I realized I forgot to pay her for the tomatoes. I felt so guilty, I couldn't eat the tomatoes. I must find Betty.

VENDOR 2: Betty from Rhinebeck Farms?

HERVÉ: Long brown hair with sun gold highlights.

VENDOR: She took the day off. Mental health.

HERVÉ: Mental health? Is she OK?

VENDOR 2: Post-traumatic stress.

HERVÉ: Do you know where I can find her? I must pay her.

VENDOR: I doubt she cares about the money. How much could you owe her?

HERVÉ: Still. It's the principle. It wouldn't be right.

VENDOR 2: If you want, I can give her the money.

HERVÉ: Thank you for the generous offer, but I would like to see her myself.

VENDOR 2: We gotcha.

45

VENDOR: That Betty's a sight for sore eyes. Very sore eyes.

HERVÉ: Yes. I want to make sure she's okay. Offer her a bear hug. A shoulder to cry on. Unconditional support.

VENDOR: Sure, sure. That's what we all want.

VENDOR 3: Speaking of support, how about supporting us?

HERVÉ: But of course! Anyone selling wine?

VENDOR: Wine for Betty?

VENDOR 3: I got wine. Cases of wine. What kind are you looking for? Red. White. Blue.

HERVÉ: Does anyone know what kind of wine Betty would like?

VENDOR 2: I bet Betty prefers Freedom wine.

VENDOR: Don't we all?

HERVÉ: *Appellation Sancerre, s'il vous plait.*

VENDOR 3: Sancerre?

HERVÉ: *Non?* Then how about a nice, crisp *Viognier*?

VENDOR: *Sancerre!*

VENDOR 3: *Viognier?*

VENDOR 2: Are you French?

HERVÉ: I thought you wanted me to buy Freedom wine.

VENDORS swarm HERVÉ, menacing.

VENDOR: It's not just an expression.

HERVÉ: Fine, forget Freedom wine, I buy something from Long Island.

VENDOR 3: We asked you a question. Are you French?

HERVÉ: Belgian.

SCENE 3

SETTING: Farmer's Market, Union Square.
AT RISE: One of the shoppers, ASIAN AMERICAN.

ASIAN AMERICAN: My grandfather used to say there's no such thing as a bad orange in California. Of course he used to say that as he tried to sell you a whole crate full of oranges. All kinds of oranges. Blood oranges. Valencias. Clementines. You can never have too much Vitamin C. You don't want to catch scurvy, do you? Scurvy. That was his favorite word. He used to cackle just saying it. Scurvy. Grandpa thought it was such a funny sounding word for something that means bleeding under the skin, bleeding gums. But scurvy ceased to be a barrel of laughs when the Japanese bombed Pearl Harbor. Suddenly my grandparents were considered high security risks and were taken away to internment camps. They lost their citrus orchard. They lost their sense of humor. So when the second plane hit, I grabbed my address book and pulled out a road map. I panicked. Where the hell am I going to go if the terrorists are Asian? Who will have the guts to protect me from illegal, immoral seizures? Do I know anyone with that kind of courage? I'm not sure I do, so I prayed to God. Please please, dear God, don't let the terrorists be Chinese, Japanese, Korean, Filipino, Vietnamese, Polynesian, anybody that remotely looks like me. Am I fucking ashamed that I jumped for joy when I learned the terrorists were Muslim? You betcha. Ideally, it shouldn't matter. Ideally, we're, above all, Americans. Ideally, it's innocent until proven guilty. Ideally, there are no bad oranges anywhere. Grandpa, you were definitely right about one thing, you can still die of scurvy. Scurvy also means worthless, mean, contemptible. Grandpa died at Manzanar, a victim of mean, worthless contempt.

SCENE 4

SETTING: Exterior Fire House, New York City. Lots of candles, posters, flowers and MOURNERS.
AT RISE: MOURNERS. Spotlight on FIREMAN's PREGNANT WIDOW.

FIREMAN'S PREGNANT WIDOW: You warned me this could happen. But you said the odds of it happening were a million to one. You said buildings are much safer than they used to be. Up to code. I can't help but wonder what you were thinking, if you were thinking, running into a building that was going to collapse on you. You probably weren't thinking. No time to spare. No time to assess the odds.

FIREMAN'S PREGNANT WIDOW (cont.): Just run into the fire. Save people. Save as many people as you can. Doesn't matter who, what, when or where. Save the people who snub you on the street when they don't know you're a fireman. Save the people who sleep like babies when they're parked illegally at a fire hydrant. Save the people who don't fucking move in heavy traffic but expect you to save their loved one. Save the people who mess with fire hydrants because they're "too hot," knowing full well that water pressure is a matter of life and death. Save anyone and everyone because that's your job. That's who you are.

A lot of people stuck in the building got to use their cell phones one last time, to say goodbye and I love you one last time. We had to watch the news. Answer a call from Mayor Rudy Giuliani. The Mayor's sorry for my loss. That's great. Fucking great. I've decided, for the baby's sake, if I remarry, my next husband has to be a coward, someone who would run from a burning building. Has to be me-first, someone who wouldn't put strangers before his wife and baby. Someone who would rather suck gas than be somebody else's hero.

SCENE 5

SETTING: High-rise, Battery Park City.
AT RISE: POLICE OFFICER stops KATIE.

POLICE OFFICER: Miss, where do you think you're going?

KATIE: I brought latte and donuts.

POLICE OFFICER: Thanks. Are you from the Red Cross?

KATIE: Sort of.

POLICE OFFICER: Let's see some ID.

KATIE: I have to find a friend. It's imperative.

POLICE OFFICER: The whole world's looking for someone. What organization are you from?

KATIE: My own? Believe me, I'm doing this out of charity.

POLICE OFFICER: I'm sorry, but haven't you been paying attention. Access is prohibited. Strictly prohibited.

KATIE: But I live below 14th, I'm not trespassing.

POLICE OFFICER: No exceptions.

KATIE: Officer, I live in this neighborhood.

POLICE OFFICER; Someone stole axes off a fire truck this morning. Can't believe we risk our lives to save perps.

KATIE: I'm not a criminal.

POLICE OFFICER: It's for your own safety. There's no power in these buildings. The smoke hasn't stopped. No idea if this building is going to come tumbling down. It's not secure.

KATIE: No electricity. You mean I'd have to walk up 40 flights of stairs?

POLICE OFFICER: Is this guy worth dying for?

KATIE: How'd you know it was a guy?

POLICE OFFICER: You got lousy boyfriend written all over you –

KATIE: He's not my boyfriend.

POLICE OFFICER: An ex.

KATIE: That would be too simple. Clear. Easy.

POLICE OFFICER: I get it, you still love him in spite of yourself.

KATIE: You don't want to know. Believe me, as an officer of the law, you really don't want to know.

POLICE OFFICER: You want my advice?

KATIE: Find some other chump to climb 40 flights of stairs?

POLICE OFFICER: Does your boyfriend have a pet? The ASPCA can help you if your boyfriend has a cat, dog, bird, goldfish, mongoose –

KATIE: Mongoose.

POLICE OFFICER: New Yorkers have the strangest pets.

KATIE: What about a snake?

POLICE OFFICER: Anything that could die without food, water, electricity.

KATIE: Knowing Connor, if he had any pets at all, he'd own a snake. Yeah, I think I'll tell the ASPCA that Connor owns a snake –

POLICE OFFICER: *(Shushing KATIE from telling a lie.)* Miss, as an officer of New York City's finest, sworn to uphold the law, to protect and to serve, may I remind you, you have the right to remain silent, you have the right to fabricate no lies.

SCENE 6

SETTING: ALEX and DANA's living room.
AT RISE: ALEX is plopped in front of the TV when DANA returns. ALEX quickly changes the channel to PBS and quickly hangs up the phone when DANA enters.

ALEX: Hey sweetheart. Where have you been? Gigi and I missed you.

DANA: Who were you on the phone with?

ALEX: Broker. Trying to preserve our portfolio. Market's taking a major nosedive.

DANA: Turn the TV off.

ALEX: But look, I turned it to your favorite station, PBS.

DANA: Now.

ALEX: Sure. What's wrong?

DANA: Have you heard from your crazy cousin Henry?

ALEX: No.

DANA: But you've tried.

ALEX: Well, I thought I better not talk to him until after we get back from Italy. To avoid any awkwardness about not using him to house-sit.

DANA: I'm curious, why does Henry steal the things I treasure the most? Why doesn't he ever steal something that breaks your heart?

ALEX: What are you talking about? He's stolen plenty of things I like. I'm just more forgiving because he's my cousin. Family.

DANA: Is he, Alex? Is Henry really your cousin? I have to ask.

ALEX: Why the Spanish inquisition?

DANA shows ALEX the poster of HENRY. ALEX GASPS.

ALEX: Oh my god, where did you get this?

50

DANA: Union Square.

ALEX: Can't be, can it?

DANA: You gave him my dress, didn't you?   My favorite dress.

ALEX: Look. Dana, we have so much. You like to shop. Every time he steals, it gives you a new space to fill.

DANA: What else did you give him?

ALEX: There are more important things than a damn dress. Especially now, Dana.

DANA: I'm talking about our marriage.

ALEX: Can't we find cousin Henry first?

DANA: Him first, me second, is that it?

ALEX: You're very much alive.

DANA: That's who you've been calling every chance you get, isn't it?

ALEX: I've been trying to reach my sponsor.

DANA: I ran into your sponsor at the blood bank.

ALEX: Thank goodness Eric's OK.

DANA: He was worried about you. Wanted to know how you were doing, how you were holding up.

ALEX: I tried plenty of times to reach Eric, his phone wasn't working for days.

DANA: He said he tried reaching you too, but our phone was always busy.

ALEX: I'm so relieved Eric's alive and well.

DANA: Have you reached Henry?

ALEX: No. Not yet.

DANA: But you've tried. Admit it.

ALEX: Yes, I've tried. Countless times. You happy now?

DANA: What reason would he have to go downtown?

ALEX: I'm not sure.

DANA: Truth, Alex.

ALEX: I don't know. *(Light bulb.)* Except…maybe --

DANA: Are you having an affair?

ALEX: Of course not. He's my cousin.

DANA: You love him.

ALEX: I love Henry the way you love Katie.

DANA: That's what I thought. Used to think.

ALEX: I love you, Dana.

DANA: Like a cousin?

ALEX: As my wife.

DANA: Nothing makes sense. It's the Twin Towers all over again.

ALEX: Dana, listen to me, I let my crazy cousin Henry take those things because when I'm with him, he makes me feel like a better person. Sounds crazy, doesn't it, but isn't that why you're so warm and generous with Katie? Somehow Katie makes you feel virtuous. Like you're more than who you are. Same thing with Henry. Henry makes me feel like a different person.

DANA: And in exchange, you gave him all my favorite things.

ALEX: I had to. Otherwise he was going to tell you I like to tell you I like to dress up in women's clothing.

DANA: What? Why haven't you told me this before?

ALEX: It's not that big a deal.

DANA: I think it is.

ALEX: What a person likes to wear? On the outside? Are we that superficial?

DANA: You wear my dresses?

ALEX: Some of them. Not all. I'm partial to silk. And linen. The natural fibers.

DANA: All the maids we hired and fired.

ALEX: I feel bad about that.

DANA: Do you wear my lingerie too?

ALEX: Please. That's unsanitary.

DANA: So you have your own.

ALEX: Not a lot. Just a few pieces. Makes me feel sexy. It's sexy on you. Why not me?

DANA: All this time, I've been hating Henry. And now he might be gone, it's so unfair. Why did you lie to me? Why?

ALEX: Think of it as a kind little white lie. A pretty lie that feels smooth to the touch.

DANA: What are we going to do?

ALEX: Dana, I love you so much it hurts. Please don't leave me over a silly dress and a pair of high heels.

DANA: You wear high heels too?

ALEX: Rarely. My back.

DANA: Jesus.

ALEX: Dana, please don't leave me.

DANA: Why not? Aren't you gay?

ALEX: No! Not all cross-dressers are gay.

DANA: How could I be so fucking blind?

ALEX: Because you and me, we're true romantics. Incurable romantics.

DANA: If you're not gay, what does it mean that you like to dress in women's clothes?

ALEX: I'm a straight man that relishes style and fashion.

DANA: I owe Henry an apology. A long apology.

ALEX: I'm sure he understands.

DANA: I feel terrible. Should we join a twelve-step program?

ALEX: What for? Cross-dressing isn't a disease, Dana.

DANA: It's not normal.

ALEX: Nothing's normal any more. Normal flew out the window a long time ago.

DANA: Still. All this time, I thought I was the one who made you a better person. More than who you are.

ALEX: And you do, most of the time, when you're not so busy, running around.

DANA: Are you saying I should stay home more?

ALEX: Now that you know, think of the new, bolder adventures we can have, shopping. Dressing up in the privacy and comfort of our own home. X-rated Romance with a capital X, capital R.

DANA: What about Henry? Where does he fit in? *Ménage à trois.*

ALEX: Come to think of it, I'm not sure I'll ever see Henry again.

DANA: Oh Alex. Don't promise what you can't keep.

ALEX: Henry's gone. Free. It's better this way. For him. For us.

DANA: Bite your tongue!

ALEX: I know cousin Henry's still alive.

DANA: Why would someone post his photograph at Union Square?

ALEX: He could have posted those himself.

DANA: Alex. Don't be heartless.

ALEX: *(With conviction and twinges of envy.)* No. Henry warned me this might happen some day. He talked about it all the time. He swore that one of these days he was just going to disappear and reinvent himself. As a woman. You did it, Henry, my hat's off to you, you broke free. May we all be so bold to follow in your footsteps. To Freedom with a Capital F.

SCENE 7

SETTING: AMTRAK STATION to Los Angeles. This scene should be staged hazily so that it's unclear if it's a dream, or reality. Is HENRY really alive, or is this ALEX's fantasy?
AT RISE: PASSENGERS boarding a train. HENRY as ANNA gathers her belongings, then stops to deliver her monologue, say goodbye to New York.

HENRY as ANNA: *(A platinum blonde transvestite.)* My darling Alex. I'm sorry to split on you like I did. I wish I could wipe away your tears and reassure you I'm still alive, that I made good on my threat. But I don't want to blow my cover. I don't want you to convince me to stay. When will I ever get another chance like this to disappear? To reinvent myself? Unlike you, I don't have much to lose. My poor family's better off without me, the shame. All my life, I have to fight for some bread, some butter. You've seen my scars. Permanent. People make it sound so easy. Be who you are. Be who you were meant to be. All that you can be. Just like the army. As if there were 12 steps. 12 easy steps. No money down. 12 easy payments. They don't tell you about the beatings. The black eyes. The ass-kickings. The mornings you just want to scrunch up and die. How many times I poured Drano in a glass. How many times I wish I could just stick my head in the oven and poof! No more.

I'm sorry I took so much. It started out as a game, to see how much power I had over you. Then I realized that I could make serious money selling your wares. Except for the dresses. I kept the dresses. I'm going to need them, more than ever now. Soon as those planes hit, I felt like those people in the Towers. Trapped. A woman trapped in a man's body. When the Towers fell, I thought, that could have been me. I could die trapped in a man's body. That's how it feels to be trapped, burning with desire, burning without an escape. I knew what I had to do. I'm headed for Los Angeles, where I will be reborn. As a woman. As Anna, the Swedish masseuse.

SCENE 8

SETTING: Amtrak Train.
AT RISE: SCREECH. Train comes to a halt. POLICE OFFICERS storm the cars and "randomly" select people to interrogate and search.

THERON: Every time the train brakes with a sudden screech, my heart shudders. The cops storm the cabins. All stern and mighty. Hiding behind their dark sunglasses so they can give us the once-over. So they can assess our terrorist quotient. By now, us dark ones, we know the drill. Sweeten that poise. Act grateful. Be complimentary. Why, thank you sir, I would love to show you the contents of my suitcase. Jonathan Franzen subversive, why no, the title *How To Be Alone*, it's the title of an essay about books. How the book-reading public is dwindling, but how books can make you feel less alone. I've got his other book here, too, *The Corrections*. I know it's thick. Heavy. Believe me, I wish it were in paperback too.

55

THERON (cont.): Oprah picked it for her Book of the Month Club. Please. Oprah? She wouldn't pick the book if it were a terrorist manifesto. No, I wasn't being sarcastic. No, I wasn't trying to imply you don't read. Sir, if I was really trying to pick a fight, I'd point out that you're as dark as I am and ask you if that irony is lost on you, or if this is just a job, or what are you thinking? No, but I can see you're in no mood for brain picking. So in that case, may I show you something else? Perhaps my clean underwear? Laundered with *Bounce*. My G*lide*? I floss after every meal. No morsels hidden between my pearly whites. No, please don't read my journal. I swear, my private thoughts have nothing to do with terrorism. The journals are more a daily digest of my struggles. Am I doing the right thing? Breaking up with Sally. Moving west. What makes me think I could interest Quentin Tarantino? Why do I have so many changes of clothing, different styles? Officer, I'm an actor. I like to look the part when I audition. I hear L.A. is a tough nut to crack. I'm trying to cover all the bases. Corporate, bohemian, sexy, effeminate, dangerous. Another look at my drivers license, sure. Sure, I'd be happy to walk down the station with you. Answer some more questions. Absolutely. I'd be honored, it's my patriotic duty. Is it all right if I bring a book?

SCENE 9

SETTING: *ALEX and DANA's penthouse has duct tape around all window and door openings. The room has been restored to its original state of*
tidiness. There is a big American flag hanging prominently, to block the view where the Towers once stood.
AT RISE: *ALEX and DANA wear pretty dresses while watching a TV sitcom. There is a loud KNOCK on the door. ALEX and DANA exchange looks, clearly not expecting anyone.*

ALEX: Did you order food?

DANA: What for? Katie made us a big pot of chicken soup.

ALEX: Are we expecting another one of Katie's friends?

DANA: Not that I know of.

ALEX: Who could it be?

DANA: There's only one way to find out.

ASPCA REP (O.S.): I hear voices. Open up, I know someone's in there.

ALEX: Where's Katie when you need her?

DANA: Flip you for the door?

DANA takes out a quarter.

ASPCA REP (O.S.): C'mon, I walked up 40 flights of stairs to bring you your special package.

ALEX: Heads.

DANA flips the quarter.

DANA: Ha, ha. Tails, you lose.

ALEX: But honey –

DANA: Don't be shy, you look marvelous.

ASPCA REP keeps on RINGING the doorbell.

ASPCA REP (O.S.): Open up.

ALEX: I'm coming.

ALEX opens the door.

ALEX: What do you want?

ASPCA REP: Hi. I'm from the ASPCA.

ALEX: Is there a problem? Are you here for Gigi? Did someone complain about Gigi?

ASPCA REP: Who or what is Gigi?

DANA: Gigi's our beloved West Highland white terrier.

ALEX: You can't have Gigi.

ASPCA REP: Relax, I'm not here for Gigi. I have some DNA samples for a Miss Katie Fields.

ASPCA REP tries to hand the DNA samples to DANA.

ASPCA REP Are you Katie Fields?

DANA: I'm not Katie Fields.

ALEX: Katie's out.

ASPCA REP: Well, will one of you sign for the DNA samples?

57

ALEX: Gross.

DANA: You're not giving us bones, or gruesome body parts?

ASPCA REP: It's just a toothbrush, a hairbrush, a razor. Ordinary stuff everyone has.

ALEX: Yeah, but this guy's dead.

ASPCA REP: You don't know that. Yet.

DANA: Chances are.

ASPCA REP: Isn't that what someone here desperately needs to confirm? Whether or not this guy's dead?

ALEX: Our houseguest. She can't rest. She makes us dizzy.

DANA: Always trying to do too much.

ASPCA REP: Don't you want to help her?

DANA: Alex offered her Valium.

ALEX: We're putting her up. We let her friends stay overnight. Use our phones. Ransack our refrigerator. Isn't that enough?

DANA: Every time you try to save the world, you lose a little bit of your self.

ASPCA REP: Look, we're all shaken, trying times, but I have more deliveries.

ALEX: Your friend, you sign.

DANA: Can't we have Katie call you and schedule re-delivery?

ASPCA REP: Do I look like UPS to you?

DANA: It's just that we don't want dead people's DNA in our house.

ALEX: No more grief.

DANA: We're trying to protect ourselves from the stench. The stench of human remains.

ALEX: We made an agreement. A romantic agreement.

ASPCA REP: The ASPCA is very short-handed. Not to mention, the victim's home had no pets. There was no snake. None. I climbed 40 flights of stairs of an unsecured building for nothing. I could fine you. Heavily.

ALEX: We'll pay the fine. No problem. How much? Dana, grab our checkbook.

DANA: Of course. We'll even tip you. Generously.

ASPCA REP: What's the big fucking deal?

ALEX: Hey. Watch your language. This is our house. We have the right to protect ourselves from the unspeakable pain.

DANA: We're trying to start over. Fresh start.

ALEX: Fresh romantic start.

DANA: We want to feel safe again. Secure.

ASPCA REP: Don't we all?

DANA: If you can't feel safe in your home, where?

ASPCA REP: Nowhere.

ALEX: We're trying to get away. Italy. And then the terrorists attacked.

DANA: We want to put all this behind us. He promised me romance.

ALEX: Romance with a capital R.

ASPCA REP: What if I leave it outside your door? In your umbrella stand.

ALEX: Fine.

DANA: What an excellent idea.

ASPCA REP: I still need someone's signature.

ALEX: Don't look at me.

DANA: What if you forge Katie's signature?

ASPCA REP: What? Make a mockery of my valor?

ALEX: I'm in A.A. and I can't afford to drink again.

DANA: Who knows what can happen if he starts drinking again. Believe me, you don't want to be held responsible.

ALEX: Are you married?

ASPCA REP: 7 years.

ALEX: Then you know, it's more than an itch. It's too embarrassing for words.

DANA: Help us resume the romance. Please.

ASPCA REP: Where's that generous donation you promised me?

ALEX: A couple thousand do?

ASPCA REP: Please. Make it out to the ASPCA. Do yourselves a favor. Get professional help.

SCENE 10

SETTING: New York and Sydney, Australia. In New York: DANA and ALEX's kitchen, dark of night. In Sydney: late afternoon/early evening the next day, BARBARA (KATIE's MOM) drinking scotch on the verandah.
AT RISE: KATIE pours herself coffee when the phone RINGS.

KATIE: *(Softly.)* Hello?

BARBARA: Good day, I'm calling long distance, from Sydney, Australia, I'm looking for Katie Fields.

KATIE: This is Katie.

BARBARA: Hello? This is Barbara Fields, calling all the way from Australia.

KATIE: Mom?

BARBARA: Katie?

KATIE: Is it really you, mom?

BARBARA: Well, I'll be. Josh said I might find you here, but I had to hear for myself. I couldn't sleep not knowing if you were dead or alive.

KATIE: Yeah. What rotten luck I have, huh?

BARBARA: You sound different.

KATIE: I'm definitely not the same person.

BARBARA: Soon as we saw it on the telly, my heart sank.

KATIE: I lost a lot of friends and former colleagues, mom.

60

BARBARA: I'm sorry, Katie. My heart bleeds for you, but thank goodness you're OK. I was so worried, I couldn't sleep.

KATIE: If I hadn't quit Wall Street to write, it could have been me up there, burning.

BARBARA: Now now, Katie, no sense dwelling over what could have been. Everything happens for a reason. And on that note, I better go.

KATIE: Go?

BARBARA: Your President Bush seems to know what he's doing.

KATIE: But Mom, isn't there more to say? Share?

BARBARA: Katie, darling, I just wanted to make sure you were OK. Now that I know you're OK, I feel a whole lot better. Thanks.

KATIE: But, mom, I'm not OK. Just because I'm alive doesn't mean I'm OK. I'm far from OK.

BARBARA: Sweetheart, get some rest. I'm sure you'll feel better in the morning. Good luck, kiddo. I wish you only the best.

KATIE: Good luck? Why did you bother calling? How do you handle the guilt, mom?

BARBARA: Scotch. Single malt.

BARBARA hangs up quickly and guzzles some scotch. KATIE starts to cry. She puts her coffee down and heads for the bathroom to wipe her eyes. ALEX tiptoes out and puts valium in her coffee. ALEX tiptoes out.

SCENE 11

SETTING: DANA and ALEX's living room, large TV is on. A week later.
AT RISE: DANA and ALEX are watching a Britcom – As Time Goes By - in their silk robes, drinking coffee. GUFFAWING.

DANA: Who knew Judi Dench could be so funny!

ALEX: I hope we're still that much in love when we're their age.

DANA: Why wouldn't we be? A little botox here, niptuck there.

ALEX: Papaya extract injections for my back.

DANA: We'll be fine.

ALEX: Good as new.

DANA: Better than new.

ALEX: New and improved.

DANA: Funny.

DANA and ALEX peck. KATIE emerges, groggy.

KATIE: Coffee?

DANA: In the kitchen. Freshly brewed.

ALEX: It's quite strong. European in nature.

KATIE: Good grief. I feel like I'm in a fog. Why do I feel so groggy this morning?

DANA: Maybe you should go back to bed. Catch some more z's.

ALEX: You look like you finally got some sleep.

DANA: Alex is right, you look refreshed.

KATIE: You know what, I think it finally caught up with me.

ALEX: We gave you some Valium.

KATIE: You did? How much? Why?

ALEX: It's not healthy to go an entire week without sleep.

DANA: Your eyes were getting puffy, Katie. Very puffy.

KATIE: So.

DANA: We were worried about you. You'll thank me later.

KATIE: You had no right to drug me without my permission.

DANA: We were doing it for your own good. You were running yourself ragged. We can't have you dropping of fatigue.

ALEX: All this running around, searching for human remains, it's not healthy. You have to try and preserve what you have. Have left.

DANA: I thought maybe you and I could spend some time together. Go to a museum. Have lunch at Rockefeller Center. Day of beauty is a joy forever.

KATIE: But I have to find more people. I have to –

DANA: Katie, we all think you've contributed more than your fair share. Done more than your duty.

ALEX: Far more.

DANA: You deserve to rest. You deserve to move on.

ALEX: We want to go back to the way it was. Before.

DANA: We want to heal.

KATIE: Who doesn't?

DANA: You can't let this jerk's father take advantage of you.

KATIE: How could I refuse? I'm his last hope.

ALEX: Bull.

DANA: Katie, you have to learn how to say no. Set boundaries. Put your foot down. Tell this Professor Madden you're sorry, but finding his asshole of a son is not your responsibility.

KATIE: What kind of person tells a father his missing son is an unworthy asshole?

ALEX: No one's asking you to be saint. Don't sink in the quicksand of your past.

DANA: You hated this guy's guts and now his guts sit in our umbrella stand. We have to ask, is that not insane? Twisted.

KATIE: I didn't always hate his guts.

DANA: Is that not a loud cry for help?

Doorbell RINGS.

ALEX: Sweet Jesus. Are you collecting more DNA? *(Adamant.)* Please, Katie, we can't take in any more DNA. No more.

KATIE: Want me to get the door?

DANA: Would you?

KATIE opens the front door. It's PROFESSOR MADDEN.

PROFESSOR MADDEN: Katie Fields.

KATIE: Yes?

PROFESSOR MADDEN: Katie. I'm Professor Madden. Connor's father.

KATIE: Professor Madden. What are you doing here?

ALEX: Speak of the devil.

DANA: We were just thinking of you. Katie has so much to tell you. Don't you, Katie?

PROFESSOR MADDEN: Yes? All good news, I hope.

KATIE: Didn't you get any of my messages?

PROFESSOR MADDEN: Oh, Katie, it feels good to be here. To finally meet you. May I please come in?

KATIE: Of course. Welcome to New York.

PROFESSOR MADDEN: I drove as fast as I could. As soon as the roads opened up.

ALEX: *(Excited.)* The roads are open?

PROFESSOR MADDEN: There are major delays, of course. Serious checkpoints. Security reasons. Understandable. But they can't shut us off forever, can they?

ALEX: Hear that, Dana?

DANA: Sure did, baby.

ALEX: We might be able to get away, after all. Really get away from all this putridness and squalor. How much do you think our penthouse is worth? Of course, maybe we shouldn't sell right away, considering.....Yes, maybe we should wait before we sell. Wait until we get back from the vacation we so desperately need.

DANA: What a godsend. We can breathe again. Finally some good news. This calls for a celebration.

ALEX: I'm going to call our travel agent. Price our options and maximize the romance.

ALEX and DANA smooch.

DANA: Hi, I'm Dana. May I offer you a tall refreshing glass of iced tea?

PROFESSOR MADDEN: That would be very kind of you, Dana. Thank you.

DANA: Katie?

KATIE: Sure.

PROFESSOR MADDEN: Oh Katie. You're even more beautiful than Connor described.

KATIE: Please. Won't you sit down?

PROFESSOR MADDEN: So what is it you have to tell me, Katie? You found him, didn't you? The whole drive north, that's what kept me going, how I willed myself awake. Connor's alive, isn't he?

KATIE: Professor Madden, I've asked around and looked everywhere.

PROFESSOR MADDEN: And?

KATIE: And I got a DNA sample which we can send to the labs.

PROFESSOR MADDEN: That's it?

KATIE: Sorry. I tried to tell you.

PROFESSOR MADDEN: Where have you looked? Who have you contacted? We have to cover all the bases. However long it takes. I'm not leaving.

KATIE: Professor Madden. As long as you're here, I wonder if you wouldn't mind taking over the search. Totally.

PROFESSOR MADDEN: You're not going to just abandon me, are you?

KATIE: The truth is –

PROFESSOR MADDEN: I think of you as my pseudo daughter-in-law.

KATIE: Dana? I could use some aspirin with my iced tea.

PROFESSOR MADDEN: Oh dear, do you have a headache?

KATIE: Pounding.

PROFESSOR MADDEN puts his hand against KATIE's forehead.

PROFESSOR MADDEN: Want me to rub your temples? I know this Mayan trick.

KATIE: Professor Madden. Please.

PROFESSOR MADDEN: Sweetheart. Please, call me Philip. We're practically related.

PROFESSOR MADDEN hugs KATIE tight. Real tight.

SCENE 12

SETTING: *St. Vincent's Hospital, New York City.*
AT RISE: KATIE and PROFESSOR MADDEN search for Connor in the hospital. They check out the unidentified patients. Up and down. The PATIENTS vary in the seriousness of their injuries.

DOCTOR: May I help you?

KATIE: Yes, we're looking for Connor Madden. Six feet tall, dark brown hair, 180 lbs, green eyes?

PROFESSOR MADDEN: I brought some photographs.

DOCTOR: Are you his sister?

KATIE: No.

DOCTOR: Then I'm sorry –

PROFESSOR MADDEN: She's his fiancée, I'm his father.

DOCTOR: Again, how may I help?

KATIE: We brought DNA.

PROFESSOR MADDEN: We're looking for my son. My only son.

DOCTOR: I understand that. But this is the intensive care unit, you can't just go barging into hospital rooms, looking for anyone you please.

PROFESSOR MADDEN: Do you have children, Doctor?

DOCTOR: I know it's hard, but isn't it more important for your son, your fiancé – if he's here -- to recuperate?

KATIE: You think there's hope.

DOCTOR: Somewhere amidst the chaos, yes. Crumbled.

PROFESSOR MADDEN: Just let us look.

DOCTOR: I can't have you interfering with the –

KATIE: All the other hospitals let us look around.

DOCTOR: Really?

PROFESSOR MADDEN: I drove all the way from Atlanta. Non-stop. You're a father's last hope.

KATIE: Don't you see, the sooner we find him, the sooner I'm off the hook.

DOCTOR: Off the hook? You think it's that easy? Come with me.

DOCTOR takes KATIE and PROFESSOR MADDEN to a patient who has a bone sticking out of his arm.

DOCTOR: Is this someone you know? Because we need to amputate.

KATIE shakes her head no. ANOTHER DOCTOR turns on a SAW and begins the amputation. The loud buzzing sound alone freaks KATIE out. She runs out of the hospital as fast as she can and pukes. PROFESSOR MADDEN stands wooden.

PROFESSOR MADDEN: *(Clipped.)* You imbecile! Connor has dark brown hair, green eyes and stands six feet tall. Don't you doctors ever bother to listen?

SCENE 13

SETTING: ROY, dressed up in business attire, on her way to a job interview.
AT RISE: ROY delivers monologue.

ROY: I've been unemployed for two years, cobbling a living through menial odd jobs. Shortly after the terrorist attack, my luck turned around. The phone started ringing. Suddenly there were a ton of openings. Jobs galore. Suddenly I'm wanted, needed, highly employable. I feel like a piece of shit, a fucking vulture, going to these job interviews, bragging about my strengths. My so-called assets. Showing off my can-do spirit. I can do that! Hell yeah, I'm resilient! I'm a big swinging dick. A positive thinker.   The glass is always half-full, baby. Self-starter nothing, I'm a tiger, ready to pounce. Pounce and profit. Arbitrage. Why do you think I changed my name from Helen to Roy? I know what gets your jaw to drop. *(Pelvic thrust.)* Cha-ching, cha-ching.

I feel like a despicable vulture, taking advantage of the dead, of the not yet identified human remains, but at the same time, I ask myself, if I don't land this job, if I don't find a way to feed myself, cover my ass, someone else will. Then where will I be? Back at McDonalds?

Shoving fast food down people's throats? Forgive me, but I hate serving Happy Meals with a plastic smile. Forgive me for my hubris, my greed.

SCENE 14

SETTING: World Trade Center, the gaping hole, smoke.
AT RISE: KATIE and PROFESSOR MADDEN view the site, covering their noses periodically, coughing.

PROFESSOR MADDEN: So this is where Connor worked.

KATIE: Yes. It was.

PROFESSOR MADDEN: And we're sure he went to work that day. Positive.

KATIE: Yes.

PROFESSOR MADDEN: He could've gone out for coffee.

KATIE: A colleague who got out saw him shortly before she left for her dentist appointment.

PROFESSOR MADDEN: Still, the one thing I know about Connor, he's very clever.

KATIE: He certainly was. Ingenious.

PROFESSOR MADDEN: Why are you using the past tense? I thought we weren't going to give up.

KATIE: This came for us in the mail. From the forensic experts.

KATIE tries to hand PROFESSOR MADDEN the envelope, but PROFESSOR MADDEN refuses to take it.

KATIE: The medical examiner positively identified a portion of Connor's hand. They want to know what you want to do with his hand, if you want it to be buried in the mass grave, or if you want to take it with you.

PROFESSOR MADDEN: Science isn't exact. Scientists make mistakes.

KATIE: It was conclusive. A 100% match. I'm sorry.

PROFESSOR MADDEN: He could've surprised us all and found a way. I know Connor.

KATIE: Professor, he worked on the 101st floor. He was trapped in the stairwell.

PROFESSOR MADDEN: I heard on the radio that some people got out alive by using their desks as surfboards. Surfing the rubble.

KATIE: You really think that's possible?

PROFESSOR MADDEN: I also heard that some people used their umbrellas as parachutes.

KATIE: Like Mary Poppins.

PROFESSOR MADDEN: *(As if confirming it's true, wishful thinking.)* Yes, you've heard it too.

KATIE: I also heard that some people were so unhappy with their lives that they took this opportunity to disappear, reinvent themselves. To wipe the slate clean.

PROFESSOR MADDEN: Yes, Connor often told me he wanted to retire early. That he didn't want to stay on Wall Street the rest of his life. That after Wall Street, he might go back to school, take some poetry classes, follow my footsteps – did he tell you I'm a distinguished professor of poetry at Emory?

KATIE: He did.

PROFESSOR MADDEN: I feel so foolish. That's where we should check next. The poetry departments at Columbia, NYU, Yale. Let's go home and make a list of all the universities and colleges in the tri-state area.

KATIE: Professor Madden.

PROFESSOR MADDEN: Philip. *(Puts his arms around KATIE.)* I could've been your father-in-law.

KATIE: Philip, I don't mean any disrespect, but Connor hated poetry. He found poetry pompous and too inaccessible. I'm surprised you didn't know that.

PROFESSOR MADDEN: Let's check back in with the hospitals.

KATIE: I can't.

PROFESSOR MADDEN: It's too painful.

KATIE: Very.

PROFESSOR MADDEN: I understand. I feel the same way. His loss is too great to bear.

KATIE: It's time to go home.

PROFESSOR MADDEN: I can't go home empty-handed. I've come all this way. I can't go home with less than what I arrived with. I can't go home with less than.

KATIE: I wish I knew how to comfort you. This is yours.

PROFESSOR MADDEN accepts the envelope.

PROFESSOR MADDEN: Come to Atlanta with me.

KATIE: Atlanta?

PROFESSOR MADDEN: We'll hold a memorial service for Connor at our house. You can speak. Help us celebrate Connor's life as we mourn –

KATIE: But –

PROFESSOR MADDEN: We can compare notes on Connor in the car. On the long drive home. You can tell me what Connor liked to do, where he liked to take you, his favorite interests. Give me all the details, no matter how seemingly mundane. I want to know more about my son. As much as I can. Please help me know my son.

KATIE: But I live in Los Angeles.

PROFESSOR MADDEN: Don't worry, I'll cover all your expenses.

KATIE: Professor Madden, I'm married. My husband Josh, he won't like it, he wants me home –

PROFESSOR MADDEN: Surely he can't be jealous of a dead man. Please. I'll talk to him for you. Your husband will understand.

KATIE: I have to write.

PROFESSOR MADDEN: Write?

KATIE: I'm a writer. Remember?

PROFESSOR MADDEN: How can you write at a time like this?

KATIE: Because I have to…. That's why I came to New York in the first place. I have to finish my novel.

PROFESSOR MADDEN: How can you be so selfish?

KATIE: Me?

PROFESSOR MADDEN: You broke my dead son's heart and now you're just going to run back to Los Angeles?

KATIE: Professor Madden, I know you're upset. I am too.

PROFESSOR MADDEN: Don't pretend to know how I feel.

KATIE: Please don't make me say what I don't want to say. Please don't make me say what can't be unsaid.

PROFESSOR MADDEN: Connor told us how you thought he wasn't good enough for you. How you made him read more books, go to more art museums, see more foreign films.

KATIE: *(Ludicrous, the idea!)* I made him do things he didn't want to do? Please, go on. This, I gotta hear.

PROFESSOR MADDEN: At first, my wife and I commended you for being such a good influence. I think everyone should do all those things. Broaden their knowledge, improve themselves. But did you have to be such a fucking nag? Could you have given him an occasional compliment? Did you have to cheat on him left and right?

KATIE: I cheated on him? Did he tell you that?

PROFESSOR: Connor loved you more than he loved himself. What's wrong with you? Couldn't you see my Connor was something special?

KATIE: Oh, I thought Connor was special. That was never the problem.

PROFESSOR MADDEN: Connor described you as a perfectionist. And when he fell short, you'd send him in a tailspin.

KATIE: Professor Madden, I'm warning you, if you don't hold your tongue –

PROFESSOR MADDEN: *(Vicious.)* If you had loved Connor back, if you had married him, he'd be alive today.

KATIE: You're right, Philip. If I had turned your son in, he might still be alive today. But he wouldn't be studying poetry, he'd be rotting in a fucking jail cell. Connor's favorite interest. Scamming people. Your son embezzled 10 million dollars but smart as he is, he made it look like I lost it speculating. A big foolish gamble. Unhedged. He knew he could blame it on me, the new girl. The chick that needed to prove herself to the guys. The prodigy who needed a big swinging dick. I made it so easy for him. I was a sitting duck.

PROFESSOR MADDEN: Vindictive liar.

KATIE: Oh, the managing director eventually figured it out. How many people own a Corvette, a Mercedes and a Porsche in the middle of Manhattan? But as our fearless leader pointed out, who is going to invest in a firm that scams people? Nobody. We couldn't tell a soul. So how does it feel, Professor Madden, to be let in on the secret? You feel especially proud of your son, now?

PROFESSOR MADDEN: Katie, please stop, I've just lost a son.

KATIE: I'm sorry Connor's dead. I'm sorry nothing can ever bring your soon back. I am. But he totally scammed you.

PROFESSOR MADDEN: The lavish gifts he bought us...*(Realizing.)* were paid for with ill-gotten gains?

KATIE: He scammed me too. I thought Connor was special. I thought I was in love with him. But he turned out to be one more greedy anonymous fuck.

PROFESSOR MADDEN: I feel so lost. Confused. Discombobulated. I can't be held accountable for my feelings.

KATIE: I'm sorry you're so full of regret and remorse, Professor Madden. Consider it a blessing in disguise because the way I see it, the way I experienced it, the way I was fucked, you're fucking lucky you didn't really know Connor. You're fucking lucky. Now if you'll excuse me, I'm getting out of here.

SCENE 15

SETTING: World Trade Center sight, still smoking.
AT RISE: JOY looks at the gaping hole, sighs, TSKS-TSKS, shakes her head, and then delivers her monologue.

JOY: What a dying shame. I'm sorry if you lost some friends in the terrorist attack, but there are some of us who believe America asked for it. It was simply a matter of time. When they found a bomb at the World Trade Center in 1993, did America wise up? Repent? Change?

Your uncle and I warned you that a greedy, godless nation is a nation bound for tragedy. I know as far as you're concerned, I'm some redneck Jesus freak you'd rather "forget" to invite to the family picnic. But how long do you think you can keep this charade up? All this conspicuous consumption. Reckless disregard for the earth's natural resources. Worshipping the false altar of money. Seduced by Sodom and Gomorrah.

JOY (cont.): How many more people have to die for you to start caring about the soul? The afterlife? That's right, it's up to you. Your uncle and I have this recurring nightmare, where the fires of hell are dancing out of control, threatening to consume the universe, tears are running down your face, you're shrieking in pain, but there's nothing I can do. Nothing. You're damned to hell, to burn in the eternal flames, all of you. Unless you change your evil ways. Unless you stop and give yourselves unto a higher power. God.

Give it up for God and let Walt Whitman comfort you. *"All goes onward and outward, nothing collapses, and to die is different from what anyone supposed, and luckier."*

SCENE 16

SETTING: ALEX and DANA's living room.
AT RISE: ALEX and DANA flip through a photo album on the couch when KATIE enters.

ALEX: Hey. Welcome home. How'd it go?

KATIE: About as well as could be expected.

DANA: That well.

ALEX: You look like you could use a hug.

KATIE: You guys are sure in a good mood.

ALEX: Dana's showing me some old photos of you two.

KATIE: Dana.

DANA: I couldn't resist.

ALEX: Dana was showing me the photo where you two pretend to be lesbians so Dana's father had to let her go on a date.

DANA: Remember my father's reaction?

KATIE: He chased us up and down the street with a broom.

ALEX: Dana said the neighbors called the police.

KATIE: Dana likes to embellish.

DANA: The neighbors were horrified.

KATIE: If only one of them had called the police.

ALEX: What a downer.

DANA: Great news, we're finally getting away.

KATIE: Me too.

DANA: You're kidding.

KATIE: I thought about what you said. About putting my foot down, setting boundaries. You're right. I can't do any more. I need to go home. See some California sun.

DANA: But, Katie, you just got here.

KATIE: I've been here for almost two weeks.

DANA: I know, but you can't count that. Not when you haven't gotten any writing done. Don't you need to finish your novel?

KATIE: I do.

ALEX: You'll finally get all the peace and quiet you need.

KATIE: That sounds too good to be true.

DANA: Alex and I, we rescheduled our trip to Italy.

KATIE: You're kidding.

ALEX: It's even cheaper than before because people are afraid to fly.

DANA: Much cheaper.

KATIE: I'll bet, I just bought a ticket on Amtrak.

DANA: Amtrak?

ALEX: How many days will that take?

KATIE: I've never been across country. I thought it might be scenic. Fun.

DANA: I bet Amtrak would let you reschedule your train ride.

KATIE: They very well might. The train I'm booked on is full. Every seat taken. People are too afraid to fly.

ALEX: We'd be willing to pay the difference if there's any penalty.

KATIE: Yeah?

DANA: Without question. It would be a pity for you to leave New York with mostly painful, smelly memories.

KATIE: That's true. I do feel weird leaving like this.

GIGI BARKS.

ALEX: Gigi's grown very fond of you.

KATIE: I was sort of looking forward to seeing Josh.

DANA: Why don't we fly him in?

ALEX: Yes, let's. Dana and I are suckers for a good romance. Capital R.

DANA: Think of how much fun you two could have in this penthouse. Just do me a big favor. Don't break our bed.

KATIE: You're making this very tempting.

DANA: What have you got to lose?

KATIE: Can't you get another house sitter?

DANA: What for?

ALEX: We want you.

KATIE: You two are so cute. Why is it so important to you that it be me?

DANA: Simple. You're my best friend in the whole wide world. The only person I can trust.

ALEX: A-hum.

DANA: After Alex.

KATIE: But Dana, after all I've been through the past two weeks –

DANA: I know it's been rough, on all of us. You're entitled to some bonafide some R & R.

KATIE: What about one of my friends that you met? They might enjoy house-sitting.

DANA: We have so much history that binds us. How many people can you say knew you way back when? You and I, we can always make new friends, but we'll never meet someone who has as much history as we do.

KATIE: But so much as changed, Dana. I'm not the same person I was in high school. I'm not even the same person I was just two weeks ago.

DANA: You haven't aged a bit.

KATIE: I never thought I'd look forward to going to L.A.

DANA: It's a great time to be in New York. The wind is blowing the smoke over to Brooklyn, people in New York are being very, very nice –

ALEX: Everyone is being extra nice and gentle. I'm proud to say I'm a New Yorker.

DANA: You can write to your heart's content. Curl up in the master bedroom, Gigi by your side.

KATIE: That does sound like a pretty picture.

DANA: So you'll do it?

KATIE: No. I'm sorry. Wait, that's not right. I'm not sorry. I can't. I'm going home.

DANA: After all I've done for you? We bent over backwards for you, letting you and your friends come and go as you please, answering your phone calls, taking messages, collecting DNA, letting all the bad news pile up on top of the layers of dust. The least you can do is –

KATIE: Leave?

DANA: Stay. Katie, I thought we were best friends. The best of friends.

KATIE: We were. We were.

SCENE 17

<u>SETTING</u>: *Amtrak train bound for Los Angeles.*
<u>AT RISE</u>: *Dining Car.*

MARY: The nerve of some people. Especially New Yorkers. Such a sense of entitlement. Ego. As if the world revolves around New York. They just assume. New Yorkers don't even bother asking. "May I sit with you?" "May I join you?" You most certainly cannot. Read my lips, New Yorker, <u>cannot</u>. My son and I are barely making it on my salary. We ate tuna fish casseroles for a year to save up for a family vacation. A year! My husband's what George Bush called a temporary unfortunate diseconomy of scale. Laid off, but does anyone give a shit? Does anyone send us truckloads of money, help us find him since he's gone missing. Do you know what it's like to reek of tuna? But my son Trevor, age 7, he asks me, Mama, don't poor people have the

right to see the world? Don't poor people get to go on a family vacation? Or, is that something we just see in the movies? A whole year
smelling like shredded fish so Trevor could see the country, really see
the country. Coast to coast. Look out the window. Feel proud to be
an American. I made Trevor memorize, "*This Land is Your Land,
This Land is My Land.*" Not that it was hard or anything, I just
wanted him to fully appreciate the journey, to understand the melody
of our sacrifice. He loved it as we flipped through the slick bro-
chures, promising scenic natural wonders. Grand Canyon. Mighty
Mississipp'. Land of Enchantment. Show me State. You know what
we've seen so far? The Missouri River at night. Rusted out cars.
Tires. Discarded computers. Dirty laundry. Hubcaps. Smokestacks.
Junkyard after junkyard. America is connected by junk. A pioneer
trail of junk. That wasn't the view we paid good money for, the view
we were promised. So fuck you if every seat is taken in the dining
car, I didn't pay to eat with fucking cowards, people who took the
train out of <u>fear</u>. I didn't spend my life savings to share my table with
some yuppie that has the nerve to think his or her destination is more
important than mine, his or her loss far deeper than mine. For god's
sake, you should show some consideration for those who have <u>always</u>
been less fortunate.
          (Singing.)
This Land is My Land. This Land is Your Land.
From California to the New York Islands
From the Redwood Forests to the Gulf Stream Waters
This Land Was Made for You and Me.
          (For emphasis.)
And Me. And <u>Me</u>.

SCENE 18

SETTING: Amtrak train.
*AT RISE: YOUNG SOLDIERS, barely 20, march up and down the
train, DRUNK as SKUNKS, rowdy, cruising for chicks, tossing empty
beer cans. ONE YOUNG SOLDIER, MACK, stops when he hears a
sexy whistle.*

YOUNG SOLDIER: I ain't afraid of no stinking Osama Bin Laden.
We gonna kick his fucking Muslim ass. Blow his fucking ass to
Mars. I ain't fucking afraid of nobody. Truth is I'm looking forward
to it. Yeah, I am. Born a fighter, I'll die a fighter. I know war is serious business. Why the fuck you think me and the guys are drinking
as much as we can before we get there? As I told that old man who
told me to shut the fuck up, hey old man, relax, you want your social
security check, well, I'm gonna secure it for you. How's that

grandpa? Save you from governmental failure to issue. The least you can do for me, is let me have my last hurrah. To cheer me on. It's like that polka song, in heaven there is no beer, that's why we drink it here. I just hope this ain't gonna turn out like fucking 'Nam where we come home and people fucking boo us. Drop their heads in shame at our service. What's that shit about? You want protection, you want your rights, your freedom to say and do as you fucking please, but you think you can get it sitting on your ass reading books? Reading books by piss-ant left wing intellectuals who sooner run to Canada than accept the responsibility and weight of their beliefs. You think you can stop terrorism by blocking traffic? Turning the other cheek? Circulating petitions? Is that how you would have prevented the Holocaust? World War I? What if the bad guys don't play by your rules? You probably voted for Al Gore and you know what, if Al Gore was President, he'd still be thinking about it and thinking about it and thinking about it. Meanwhile, a terrorist with a bomb is in your house, sits on your bus, fires an AK-47 through your front window, kills your baby, then what? You want to think about it? You gonna offer him fucking a Diet Coke and say, hey, let's talk it out. Tell each other dirty jokes. Draw up a peace treaty. Bond. Fucking bullshit. Please, don't desecrate my uniform. Is there not a point in your life that you would fight? No, not me. I'm asking you. You personally. Think about it. What does it take to get you off your high and mighty ass and fight? Chew on that. Long and hard. In case I don't come back. Now, how about a beer? Anyone willing to buy me a beer? An American beer.

SCENE 19

SETTING: Amtrak train.
AT RISE: Amtrak pulls into Union Square, Los Angeles.

KATIE: My parents met on a train. My father was attracted to my mother because she was slightly overweight. Pleasingly plump. He liked women with an appetite and weren't afraid to show it. My dad also thought my mother was rich, because she had enough to eat. He was wrong, but by the time he found out otherwise, he was smitten.

When my parents publicly announced that someday there were going to America, everyone laughed at them. How are you two peasants, about to be three, going to get there? Magic brooms? But they were united by the Great American Dream.

Then one day a letter arrived from Kent State University. Offering my father a full-ride scholarship. My parents had never heard of Kent

State. Ohio. But hey, this was our ticket to America. Land of up-ward mobility. A dream come true. So we took off. Landed smack dab in the middle. Middle west. Middle of America.

The day after we arrived, 4 dead in Ohio. Shot by the National Guardsman. My father was standing right there. Kissinger called it "a shock wave that brought the nation and its leadership close to the point of physical exhaustion." According to my mom, the lights went out in my father that day. He began to fade. He never recovered from what he saw, from the shame, the betrayal.

I was so young, too young, but even then, I knew it was my job to do whatever I could to make their trip to America to seem worth the heartache. My job was to help us hang on. Cheer up, mommy, daddy, our life is going to improve because one day soon I'm going to buy you nice things. A nice house that doesn't rumble next to the freeway. A nice car that doesn't give out on the exit ramp on Thanksgiving. Don't believe me? Just watch me. I can do tricks. No hands. I spent every day after school at the library, immersed in the Great American Dream.

Then one day, I grabbed my babysitting money, dressed in my mother's clothes and taxied to the local Merrill Lynch office. I was 15 going on 30, so I pounded my fist on that table and said, "<u>buy</u>." Buy America. As much as I can afford. Give it to me.

Do I miss Wall Street? Do I miss the bold glistening Twin Towers that stood up to the sky, rain or shine? Of course I do. I miss my friends and family. I miss the days where I was so naïve I thought I could keep the world from caving in, if only I had the money, the drive. I miss the days when there was no shame in hunger. I miss the Great American Dream.

<u>END OF PLAY</u>

NOTES